4

D1423914

DEPARTMENT

Modelling with rigid bodies

The School Mathematics Project

CAMBRIDGE
UNIVERSITY PRESS

Main authors   Janet Jagger
Ann Kitchen
Tom Roper

Team leader   Ann Kitchen

Project director   Stan Dolan

The authors would like to give special thanks to Ann White for her help in preparing this book for publication.

Cartoons by Paul Holland

Photographs by Ann and Ken Kitchen

Published by the Press Syndicate of the University of Cambridge
The Pitt Building, Trumpington Street, Cambridge CB2 1RP
40 West 20th Street, New York, NY 10011-4211, USA
10 Stamford Road, Oakleigh, Victoria 3166, Australia

© Cambridge University Press 1993

First published 1993

Produced by 16-19 Mathematics and Laserwords, Southampton

Printed in Great Britain by Scotprint Ltd., Musselburgh.

ISBN 0 521 42643 X

Contents

1 Forces and couples

1.1 Introduction

In *Modelling with force and motion* you found that the particle model was not always suitable for rigid bodies. This unit considers a different model, one which can be applied to rigid bodies in both static and dynamic situations. It is referred to as the rigid body model.

A rigid body is an extended body which is fixed in size and shape. If a body is modelled as a particle, the forces acting on it are concurrent, whereas for an extended body you found that the points of application of the forces were as important as their magnitudes.

Consider a heavy rod on a smooth table with two forces of magnitude P acting as shown in the plane of the table.

The sum of the forces is zero, but the rod will start to turn and so is not in equilibrium.

> **What extra condition is needed for a rigid body to be in equilibrium?**

Example 1

A uniform ladder of length 4 metres and weight 200 newtons rests against a smooth vertical wall with its foot on rough horizontal ground, making an angle of 60° with the ground.

(a)   Find the magnitude of the normal contact force which the wall exerts on the top of the ladder.

(b)   If the coefficient of friction between the foot of the ladder and the ground is $\frac{1}{2}$, is it possible for a man of weight 700 newtons to climb to the top of the ladder without it slipping?

Solution

(a)

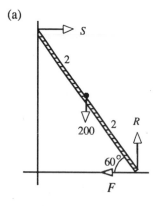

Set up a model

Let **S** newtons and **R** newtons be the normal contact forces between the ladder and the wall and floor respectively. The friction force at the wall is zero and that at the floor is **F** newtons. Assume that the ladder is a uniform rod and is in equilibrium.

Analyse the problem

To find S, take moments about an axis through the foot of the ladder.

$$S \times 4 \sin 60° - 200 \times 2 \cos 60° = 0$$

$$\Rightarrow \qquad\qquad S = 57.7$$

The contact force on the top of the ladder is 57.7 newtons.

(b)

Set up a model

Represent the man by a particle of weight 700 newtons placed d metres from the foot of the ladder.

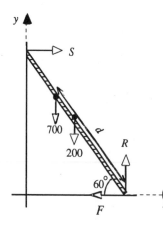

Analyse the problem

The ladder is in equilibrium, so the sum of the forces is zero.

$$\begin{bmatrix} S \\ 0 \end{bmatrix} + \begin{bmatrix} -F \\ 0 \end{bmatrix} + \begin{bmatrix} 0 \\ R \end{bmatrix} + \begin{bmatrix} 0 \\ -700 \end{bmatrix} + \begin{bmatrix} 0 \\ -200 \end{bmatrix} = 0$$

$$\Rightarrow \quad S = F \quad \text{and} \quad R = 900$$

Taking moments about the foot of the ladder

$$S \times 4 \sin 60° - 700\,d \cos 60° - 200 \times 2 \cos 60° = 0$$

$$S = \frac{350d + 200}{3.464} = F$$

2

For static equilibrium $F \leq \mu R$, so

$$\frac{350\,d + 200}{3.464} \leq \frac{1}{2} \times 900$$

$$350\,d \leq 1559 - 200$$

$$d \leq 3.88 \text{ (to 3 s.f.)}$$

Interpret / Validate

It is not possible for the man to climb to the top of the ladder. Limiting friction will be reached when he is 3.88 metres along the ladder. After this, the ladder will slip at the ground. However, in reality he is unlikely to want to stand on the very top rung. It depends what is meant by the top of the ladder.

> **In reality, the wall is unlikely to be completely smooth.**
> **How does this affect the validity of the model?**
> **You might like to experiment with a ruler and some**
> **masses.**

Exercise 1

1. A uniform ladder of weight W newtons and length 4 metres rests against a smooth vertical wall with its foot on rough horizontal ground. If the coefficient of friction at the ground is $\frac{1}{2}$, what is the minimum angle of inclination of the ladder to the ground?

2. A walking stick of weight 5 newtons and length 1 metre rests against the rail of a hatstand as shown.

    The stick makes an angle of $60°$ with the horizontal and the rail is 0.75 metre above the base of the stand. If contact with the rail is rough and that with the base is smooth, find the coefficient of friction necessary to maintain equilibrium.

3. A circular table has four vertical legs positioned at its circumference at the corners of a square. The table weighs 50 newtons. What is the least mass placed on the edge of the table which will cause it to topple over?

4. A hose-reel rests on a horizontal lawn and the hose is pulled horizontally in the direction shown.

By taking moments about the line through the point of contact with the ground, discuss which way the hose-reel will roll. In which direction should the hose be pulled to make the reel roll the other way?

5. A uniform ladder of length 2 metres and weight 200 newtons rests against a smooth vertical wall at one end and rough, horizontal ground at the other. The angle of inclination to the horizontal is 60°. If a man of weight 1000 newtons has to be able to climb to the top of the ladder, what is the minimum value of the coefficient of friction?

6. A cotton reel is held in equilibrium on a rough, inclined plane by a force of magnitude T newtons, applied tangentially to the reel up the plane at the point diametrically opposite the point of contact. If the weight of the reel is W newtons and the angle of inclination of the plane is α, find the magnitude of the force maintaining equilibrium and the minimum value of the coefficient of friction.

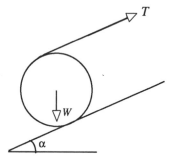

7. A uniform plank of length $2l$ metres and weight W newtons lies on rough, horizontal ground. The plank is to be raised at one end by means of a rope attached to that end and pulled to keep a constant angle α to the vertical.

How large must the coefficient of friction μ be to prevent slipping at the other end?

4

1.2   Normal contact forces and rigid bodies

A workman wants to slide a filing cabinet across the floor.

(a)   Should he push it or pull it?

(b)   What might happen when he tries to move it?

(c)   Will it matter if the cabinet drawers are empty or full?

(d)   If only one drawer is full, which one should it be to ensure the greatest stability?

Example 2

The packing case in the diagram weighs 300 newtons. A force of magnitude 30 newtons is applied as shown. Calculate the position of the line of action of the normal contact force between the floor and the packing case, assuming that the packing case is in static equilibrium.

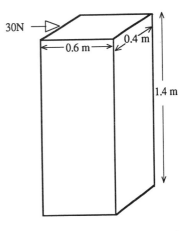

Solution

| Set up a model |

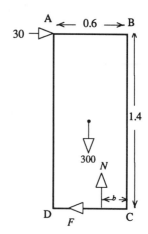

Assume that the centre of mass of the
packing case is at the mid-point.
Taking a section through the packing
case containing the centre of mass,
the forces acting, measured in newtons,
are as shown.
Let the normal contact force act at a
distance b metres from the line BC.

| Analyse the problem |

The packing case is in static equilibrium, so the vector sum of the forces is zero.

$$\begin{bmatrix} 30 - F \\ N - 300 \end{bmatrix} = 0$$

$$F = 30 \quad \text{and} \quad N = 300$$

The packing case is in static equilibrium, so the sum of the moments about any axis
through the plane of the section is zero.

Taking moments clockwise about C,

$$30 \times 1.4 + 300b - 300 \times 0.3 = 0 \qquad \qquad \text{①}$$

$$b = 0.16$$

| Interpret |

The line of action of the normal contact force is 16 cm from the edge of the section BC
and parallel to it. The value of the friction force does not affect the position of the line
of action of the normal contact force as long as it is great enough to stop the case
sliding. Equation ① shows that if you increase the push, b decreases and the line of
action of the normal force gets nearer to BC.

> The line of action of the contact force **R**, where **R** = **N** + **F**,
> passes through the mid-point of AB. Why is this?

Exercise 2

1. A filing cabinet weighs 400 newtons and is pushed as shown by a force of 100 newtons. Assuming that the cabinet is in static equilibrium and is of uniform density, find the position of the line of action of the normal contact force.

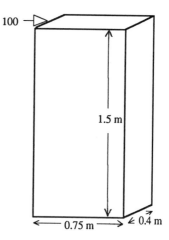

100

1.5 m

0.75 m → ↙ 0.4 m

2. A packing case of uniform density, with dimensions as shown, has a weight **W** newtons and is subject to the force **P** newtons.

    As the magnitude of the force increases from zero to its maximum value P_{max}, describe how the position of the line of action of the normal contact force changes, assuming that the packing case does not slide or topple.

    Calculate the position of the line of action of the normal contact force along AB from B when:

    (a) $P = 0$;

    (b) $P = P_{max}$;

    (c) $P = \frac{1}{2}P_{max}$.

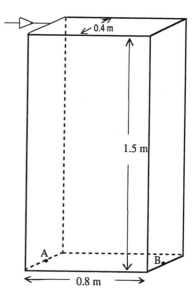

P

0.4 m

1.5 m

A   B

0.8 m

1.3   Couples

The diagram that you have been using to model the forces acting on a packing case, or similar object, in static equilibrium is given below.

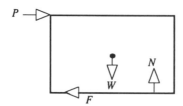

There are two pairs of forces which are equal in magnitude, but opposite in direction. **P** and **F** are one pair, **W** and **N** the other. Such pairs of forces are called **couples.** The static equilibrium can be viewed as a balance between these two pairs of forces; each pair has a turning effect, but no resultant force.

The properties of a couple are investigated in Tasksheet 1.

 TASKSHEET 1 – *Couples*

A system of two forces of equal magnitude and opposite direction is called a *couple*. A couple has no resultant force but does exert a turning effect called the moment of the couple (often called its torque).

If each force is of magnitude *F* newtons acting as shown and the lines of action are a distance *d* metres apart, then the moment of the couple is *Fd* newton-metres anticlockwise about any axis at a right angle to its plane.

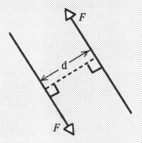

In a force diagram, such a torque can be represented as shown below, where $C = Fd$.

Example 3

Forces act as shown along the edges of a rectangle ABCD where AB = 6 metres and BC = 10 metres.

Find the magnitude and direction of the resultant couple.

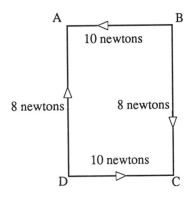

Solution (1)

Clockwise moment of the couple formed by the 8 newton forces $= 8 \times 6$
$= 48$ Nm

Anticlockwise moment of the couple formed by the 10 newton forces $= 10 \times 10$
$= 100$ Nm

Resultant couple $= 100 - 48 = 52$ Nm anticlockwise.

Solution (2)

Taking moments about an axis through A, anticlockwise:

The couple is $10 \times 10 - 8 \times 6 = 52$ Nm anticlockwise.

Exercise 3

1. Forces of 3 newtons, 5 newtons, 3 newtons and 5 newtons act along the sides PQ, QR, RS and SP respectively of a square, each side of the square being 2 metres in length. Find the resultant couple.

2. A swing door is 0.75 metre wide. The return spring provides a torque of 15 Nm which acts to close the door. What is the least force required to push the door open?

3.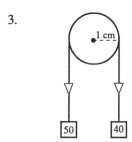

   A pulley is of radius 1 cm, and has two masses of 50 grams and 40 grams suspended over it by means of light cotton. The bearings of the pulley are rough and provide a frictional couple opposing motion. The system is stationary. Calculate the size of the frictional couple acting on the pulley.

4. A frictional couple of magnitude 3 Nm prevents a pulley from rotating. If the diameter of the pulley is 30 cm, find the necessary difference in tensions on the two sides of a rope over the pulley to start it moving.

1.4   Resultant forces and couples

You already know how to find the resultant force acting upon a particle by finding the vector sum of all the forces acting upon it.

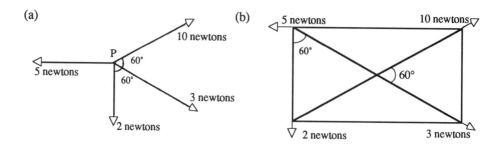

(a)

(b)

(a)   **Find the resultant force acting on the particle.**

(b)   **The same forces are acting on this lamina, which has the same mass as the particle.**

Why might the effect be different from that in (a)?

The system of forces in (b) is a system of coplanar forces, forces whose lines of action are in the same plane. Their precise effect is not immediately clear. If they could be combined (reduced) in some way, their effect would be more apparent. This is similar to reducing all the forces acting on a particle to a single resultant force. To see how a system of coplanar forces might be 'reduced' in some way consider the following simple cases.

Consider a rod with two equal forces acting on its ends.

The resultant force is of magnitude $2P$ downwards, but what is its line of action?

The line of action of the resultant force passes through the mid-point of the rod AB. (You can check this by balancing a weighted rod on your finger.)

It is important that the line of action of the force is specified precisely.

Now suppose that one of these forces is acting in the opposite direction.

In this case the resultant force is zero, but there is a couple of magnitude $P \times AB$, clockwise about any point in the plane.

These two examples suggest that a coplanar system of forces might be capable of reduction to either:

    (a)   a resultant force whose line of action must be specified;

or   (b)   a couple;

or   (c)   a combination of (a) and (b).

   TASKSHEET 2 — *Forces about a pivot*

You saw in the tasksheet that any force acting on a rigid body can be replaced by a force through an arbitrary point in the body together with a couple. The same procedure can be followed for all the forces acting in a coplanar system. All the forces may then be combined to find the resultant force which will act at the arbitrarily chosen point, and similarly all the couples may be combined to find the resultant couple.

This provides a very powerful tool in those situations where you do not know exactly what the forces are and where their lines of action are. For example, the forces in a hinge are unknown but you may confidently model them by a resultant force and a resultant couple.

> Any system of coplanar forces acting on a rigid body can, in general, be replaced by a single force acting at an arbitrary point in the plane of the forces together with a couple. Either the force or the couple may be zero.

Example 4

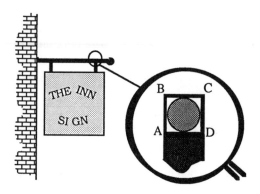

An inn sign is hung from a circular rod by two brackets. The forces on the rod due to one of the brackets can be modelled as forces of 1, 2, 3 and 4 newtons acting along the sides BA, AD, DC and CB of a square, in the directions indicated by the order of the letters. Reduce this system of forces to a force acting at B and a couple.

Solution

The original system:

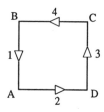

After the introduction of the necessary couples:

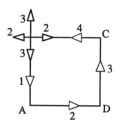

Taking axes parallel to BC and AB:

$$\text{Resultant force } \mathbf{R} = \begin{bmatrix} -4 \\ 0 \end{bmatrix} + \begin{bmatrix} 2 \\ 0 \end{bmatrix} + \begin{bmatrix} 0 \\ -1 \end{bmatrix} + \begin{bmatrix} 0 \\ 3 \end{bmatrix}$$

$$= \begin{bmatrix} -2 \\ 2 \end{bmatrix}$$

i.e. $2\sqrt{2}$ newtons acting at B in the direction DB.

The resultant couple $\mathbf{G}$ = 2 x AB + 3 x BC

= 5AB Nm anticlockwise

Example 5

ABCD is a square of side 2 metres, P is the mid-point of AD and Q is the mid-point of CD. Forces of magnitudes 10, 10, 30 and 40 newtons act along AB, CD, QB and CP in the directions indicated by the order of the letters. Find the resultant force and the position of its line of action.

Solution

Set up a model

Let the resultant force be R newtons acting at an angle α to CB as shown.

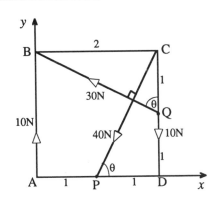

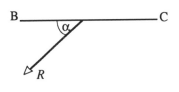

Analyse the problem

Taking axes parallel to AD and AB.

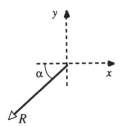

$$R = \begin{bmatrix} 0 \\ 10 \end{bmatrix} + \begin{bmatrix} 0 \\ -10 \end{bmatrix} + \begin{bmatrix} -30 \sin\theta \\ 30 \cos\theta \end{bmatrix} + \begin{bmatrix} -40 \cos\theta \\ -40 \sin\theta \end{bmatrix}$$

$\tan\theta = 2$ so $\sin\theta = \dfrac{2}{\sqrt5}$ and $\cos\theta = \dfrac{1}{\sqrt5}$.

$$R = \begin{bmatrix} -20\sqrt5 \\ -10\sqrt5 \end{bmatrix} = \begin{bmatrix} -44.72 \\ -22.36 \end{bmatrix}$$

Magnitude of $R = \sqrt{(44.72^2 + 22.36^2)} = 50$ to 2 s.f.

$$\tan\alpha = \frac{10\sqrt5}{20\sqrt5} = \frac{1}{2}$$

The force has magnitude 50 newtons and acts at an angle of 26.6° to CB below CB.

The line of action of the resultant force **R** is such that the moment of **R** about any point in the plane is the same as the sum of the moments of the separate forces about the same point.

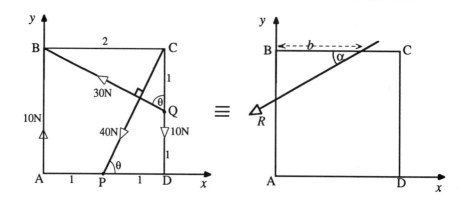

It is easiest to take moments about B or C because two of the forces pass through each of these points.

Taking moments about B:

$$10 \times 2 + 40 \times 2 \sin \theta = Rb \sin \alpha$$

$$20 + \frac{160}{\sqrt{5}} = 50b \sin 26.6°$$

$$\Rightarrow b = 4.1$$

The line of action of the force cuts BC produced at a distance 4.1 metres from B.

Exercise 4

1. Forces of magnitude 1, 2, 3 and 4 newtons act along the sides AB, BC, CD and DA respectively of a square ABCD. Reduce this system of forces to a resultant force acting through A and a couple.

2. With the forces on ABCD as in question 1, find the line of action of the resultant force so that there is no couple.

3. A triangular lamina ABC is marked out as shown in the diagram.

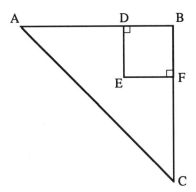

AB = BC = 3 metres and DBFE is a square of side 1 metre.
Forces are applied to the lamina:
1 newton along DB, 2 newtons along BF, 3 newtons along FE, 4 newtons along ED and 2√2 newtons along AC.

What is the resultant of this system?

4. The triangle ABC is equilateral and forces of magnitude 4, 2 and 4 newtons act along the sides AB, AC and BC respectively. Find the magnitude, direction and line of action of the resultant force.

5. Three coplanar forces acting on a rigid body can be represented in magnitude, direction and line of action by the three sides of a triangle taken in order. Show that they are equivalent to a single couple whose moment is represented by twice the area of the triangle.

 TASKSHEET 3 – *Moving bridges*

After working through this chapter you should:

1. understand that a rigid body is in equilibrium if and only if the resultant force on the body is zero **and** the sum of the moments about any point is zero;

2. be able to use the conditions of equilibrium to determine unknown forces and other variables in a given situation;

3. understand that when two bodies are in contact, the line of action of the contact force does not necessarily pass through the centre of gravity of either body;

4. understand that a couple

   - is a pair of equal but opposite forces,
   - has moment which is the same about any point in its plane,
   - is equal to the product of the magnitude of the forces and the perpendicular distance between their lines of action;

5. know that the turning effect of a couple is often called its torque;

6. be able to use your knowledge of couples and forces to reduce a system of forces acting on a rigid body to either

   - a resultant force acting through a specified point and a couple, or
   - a resultant force whose line of action is chosen such that the couple is zero;

7. be able to model real situations using moments and couples.

Couples

1.   A lamina is subject to forces as shown.

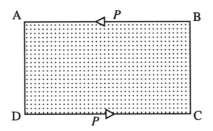

What will be the effect?

2.   Using a postcard as a model for a lamina, pierce each corner and thread string or cotton along sides BA and DC. Using the strings to exert equal and opposite forces along BA and DC, see if you can confirm your prediction of question 1.

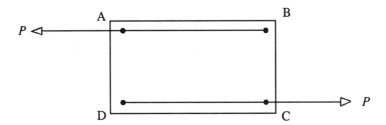

(continued)

3.

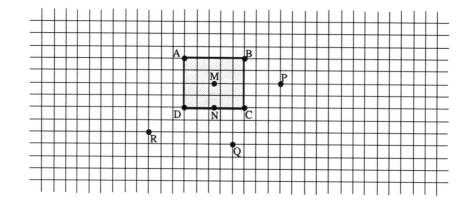

A rectangular lamina with sides 5 metres and 4 metres is placed at ABCD and two forces each of magnitude 6 newtons act along $\overrightarrow{AB}$ and $\overrightarrow{CD}$.

Calculate the moment of this system of forces about the point A. Repeat for the points D, N, M, P, Q and R. What do you notice?

4.   O is a point in the plane of two equal but opposite forces of magnitude P. By drawing a perpendicular from O to the lines of action of the forces, calculate the moment of the system of forces about an axis through O. What can you deduce from this result?

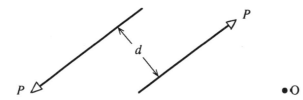

Forces about a pivot

Case (i)

OABC is a rectangular lamina with a force of magnitude P acting along AB.

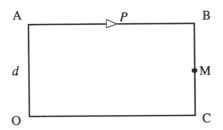

Case (ii)

As Case (i), but two forces equal in magnitude to P but opposite in direction are introduced at O. Their lines of action are parallel to AB.

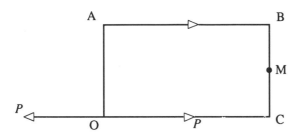

1. What is the resultant force in:

    (a) Case (i);   (b) Case (ii)?

2. Find the sum of the moments of the forces in each case about a pivot at:

    (a) O;

    (b) A;

    (c) M, the mid-point of BC;

    (d) I, any point inside OABC;

    (e) E, any point outside OABC.

3. Is the second system of forces equivalent to the first?

(continued)

In effect, the force P through A in Case (i) has been replaced by a similar force through O and a couple whose moment is Pd clockwise.

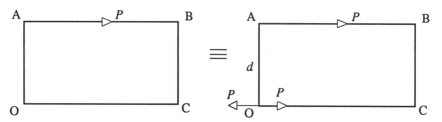

4.   Copy and complete the force diagrams on the right so that they are equivalent to those on the left. State the magnitude and line of action of the resultant force and the moment of the couple.

(a)

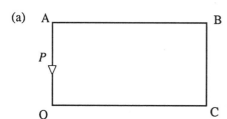

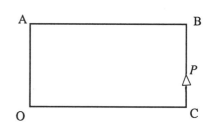

(b)

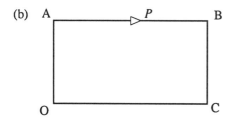

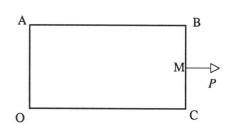

(c)

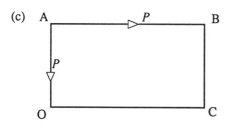

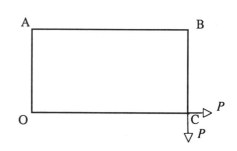

Moving bridges

Everyone is familiar with the great suspension bridges and cantilever bridges used to carry traffic over rivers, railways and other roads. You must also know of the drawbridges used on old fortifications to deny access to unwanted visitors.

The simplest drawbridges were wooden walkways that were pivoted at one end and could be pulled up by means of chains or ropes. They needed a great deal of effort to raise them in time of danger. Even more care was needed when lowering them to avoid damage caused by too rapid a descent.

For this reason some drawbridges were pivoted on a central pier so that they were balanced in equilibrium in any position. A heavy weight lowered on one end caused the bridge to lift quickly and effortlessly and the weight could be raised slowly when the bridge had to be lowered. Most drawbridges have now disappeared but their remains can be seen.

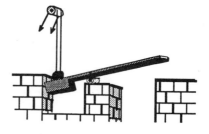

(continued)

The moveable bridges that can be seen in several of the paintings of Vincent van Gogh are interesting. They are called balance-beam bridges or portal drawbridges. They were very popular in Holland, where people had to be able to cross the network of canals easily without impeding the passage of barges.

Some form of lifting bridge was needed, but the drawbridge was cumbersome and difficult to operate. A bridge with a counterbalance provided the answer. The basic design consisted of the wooden walkway and two towers. Instead of ropes passing directly to the end of the walkway from the top of the towers, long balance beams with counterweights were pivoted at the tops of the towers and ropes passed from these to the walkway. This meant that the bridge was in equilibrium at every position so that very little effort was needed to raise and lower the bridge. Such bridges are still in use today on many canals and waterways in England, from the Shropshire Union canal near Wrenbury to the old dock basins near Tower Bridge in London.

(continued)

By altering the position of the counterweight the bridge can be designed so that it has a braking tendency when fully open or when fully closed. This reduces the likelihood of a gust of wind bringing the bridge crashing down on a barge if it is left open, or opening suddenly just as a farmer is about to drive his car across.

Problem

How big should the counterweight be so the bridge is in equilibrium in any position?

1.   Set up a simple model. (Draw a diagram and list necessary variables and any simplifying assumptions you may have made.)

2.   Carry out the analysis.

3.   Interpret your answers. Set up a simple experiment to validate these results.

4.   Discuss the effect that your simplifying assumptions have had on the validity of your solution.

Tutorial sheet

1. Forces of magnitude 3 newtons, 4 newtons and 5 newtons act along the sides AB, BC and CA of an equilateral triangle of side 1 metre. Find the magnitude and direction of the resultant force and state where its line of action cuts the line through BC.

2.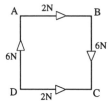

    Four forces act on a square lamina ABCD of side 2 metres, as shown. Reduce this system of forces to a single force acting at A and a couple.

3.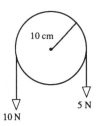

    A large pulley has masses of 1 kg and 500 grams suspended on it by a rough string. If the pulley does not start to rotate, find the minimum frictional couple in the bearings.

4. A uniform ladder leans against a smooth wall with its foot on rough horizontal ground. It is about to slip when its angle to the horizontal is 32°. What is the coefficient of friction between the ladder and the ground?

5.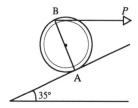

    A reel of telephone cable of weight 1000 N is held on a rough slope of angle of inclination 35° by a horizontal force of magnitude P newtons. The force acts through B where AB is the diameter perpendicular to the slope.

    Find the value of the coefficient of friction if the reel is about to slip downwards.

2 Toppling or sliding?

2.1 Introduction

In certain situations, the stability of an object is very important. Some of the glasses on the tray in the picture will be much more likely to tip over than others.

TASKSHEET 1 – *Toppling*

Example 1

The cabinet is pushed with a horizontal force at a height h metres above the floor as shown. If you want the cabinet to slide but not topple, find the relationship between h and the coefficient of friction between the cabinet and the floor.

Solution

Let the cabinet be modelled as a uniform cuboid
of width $2a$ metres and height $2b$ metres.
Let its weight be W newtons as shown.
Let the normal contact force be N newtons
acting a distance d metres from the corner A,
the friction be F newtons and the push be
P newtons.

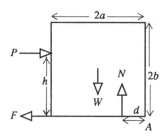

Analyse the problem

If the cabinet does not topple then $N = W$ and there is no resultant moment.

Taking moments clockwise about A, $Ph + Nd - Wa = 0$

$$\text{so } P = \frac{Wa - Nd}{h}$$

$$P \leq \frac{Wa}{h}$$

The cabinet will slide when $F = \mu N = \mu W$ and $F < P$.

So $\mu W < P \leq \frac{Wa}{h}$

Interpret

The cabinet will slide and not topple if $\mu < \frac{a}{h}$. The higher up that you push, the
smaller the coefficient of friction must be if the cabinet is not to topple.

Exercise 1

1.   A uniform solid cube of side $2a$ is placed on a rough plane which is initially
     horizontal and is then gradually inclined.   The coefficient of friction
     between the plane and the cube is μ. Find the condition on μ if the cube is
     to topple before it slides when:

     (a)   two edges of the face of the cube in contact with the plane are parallel to
           the line of greatest slope of the plane;

     (b)   a diagonal of the face of the cube in contact with the plane is parallel to
           the line of greatest slope of the plane.

2. A uniform solid cone and a uniform solid cylinder of the same height h and base radius r are placed with their plane circular faces on a rough horizontal plane. The angle θ of the plane to the horizontal is increased gradually. The plane is rough enough to prevent sliding. It is found that the cylinder topples when $\theta = \alpha$, the cone topples when $\theta = \beta$ where $\tan \beta = 2 \tan \alpha$. What can you deduce about the centre of gravity of the cone?

3.

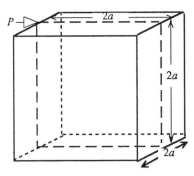

A cabinet of weight W newtons is pushed at the top by a horizontal force of P newtons. Find the conditions on μ, the coefficient of friction between the cabinet and the floor, which determine whether it will slide or topple as P is gradually increased.

4.

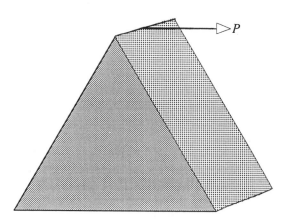

A prism has a cross-section which is an equilateral triangle.

A gradually increasing force P is applied as shown.

Show that the prism will slide before it tilts if the coefficient of friction between it and the horizontal plane is less than $\frac{1}{3} \sqrt{3}$.

2.2   Centres of mass and centres of gravity

If you wish to know whether a solid object will topple or slide, you need to know where its centre of gravity is. The purpose of this section is to enable you to be able to calculate the position of the centre of gravity.

Consider two particles of masses m_1 and m_2 positioned with respect to an origin O as shown below.

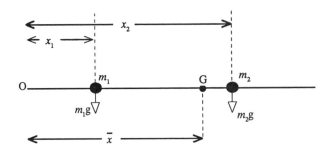

The centre of gravity is that point through which the resultant weight acts. Suppose this is at G, distance $\bar{x}$ from O.

The resultant weight is $(m_1 + m_2)g$ acting vertically downwards at G. The moment of the resultant weight about O must be equal to the sum of the moments of the separate weights about O. (This is often known as 'The principle of moments'.)

Taking moments about O, $(m_1 + m_2)\, g\,\bar{x} \;=\; m_1\, g\, x_1 + m_2\, g\, x_2$

$$\bar{x} \;=\; \frac{m_1 x_1 + m_2 x_2}{m_1 + m_2}$$

You will notice that the position of G is independent of g, the gravitational force per unit kilogram. It is therefore also referred to as the centre of mass. The positions of the centres of mass and gravity are indistinguishable in this case.

> **Are the centres of gravity and mass always at the same position?**
>
> (a)   Re-work the example above with two weights $m_1 g_1$ and $m_2 g_2$, where g_1 and g_2 are the gravitational forces per unit kilogram for the masses m_1 and m_2 respectively, and $g_1 \neq g_2$. (You may assume that the vectors g_1 and g_2 are still parallel.)
>
> (b)   Can you imagine circumstances where $g_1 \neq g_2$?

If a body is not in a constant gravitational field, the centre of gravity and the centre of mass will not coincide. For most practical purposes in the everyday world they can be considered as the same. In Chapter 5 you will see why you may need to distinguish between the centre of mass and the centre of gravity.

The definition of the centre of mass can be extended for more than two particles. For a collection of particles in space of masses $m_1, m_2, \ldots m_n$ with position vectors $\mathbf{r}_1, \mathbf{r}_2, \ldots \mathbf{r}_n$, respectively,

$$(m_1 + m_2 + \ldots m_n)\,\bar{\mathbf{r}} = m_1\,\mathbf{r}_1 + m_2\,\mathbf{r}_2 + \ldots + m_n\,\mathbf{r}_n$$

Thus, $M\,\bar{\mathbf{r}} = \displaystyle\sum_{i=1}^{n} m_i\,\mathbf{r}_i$

where M is the total mass of the particles.

$$M\bar{\mathbf{r}} = \sum_{i=1}^{n} m_i\,\mathbf{r}_i$$

In question 2 of Exercise 1, you found that the centre of mass of a uniform solid cone appeared to be one quarter of its vertical height from the circular base. This can be confirmed by direct calculation, using the ideas above.

Since the cone is symmetrical, the centre of mass will lie on its axis, so let this be the x-axis in the chosen coordinate system. The cone is then divided up into suitable pieces whose centres of mass lie on the x-axis. This suggests the use of thin slices whose planes are at right angles to the x-axis.

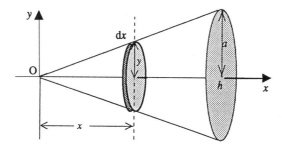

Each slice is so thin that it can be regarded as a circular disc.

Volume of disc $= \pi y^2\,\mathrm{d}x$

Mass of disc $= \rho\pi y^2\,\mathrm{d}x$, where ρ = mass per unit volume

Let the centre of mass be a distance $\bar{x}$ from O.

Then, using $\quad M\,\bar{\mathbf{r}} = \sum\limits_{i=1}^{n} m_i \mathbf{r}_i$,

$$\sum_{x=1}^{n} \rho\,\pi\,y^2\,dx\ \bar{x} = \sum_{x=1}^{n} \rho\,\pi\,y^2\,x\,dx$$

Taking limits as $dx \to 0$ and recognising ρ and π as constants,

$$\int_0^h y^2\,dx\ \bar{x} = \int_0^h xy^2\,dx$$

But $y = \dfrac{a}{h}\,x \Rightarrow y^2 = \dfrac{a^2}{h^2}\,x^2$ where a and h are constant, and so:

$$\int_0^h \frac{a^2}{h^2}\,x^2\,dx\ \bar{x} = \int_0^h \frac{a^2}{h^2}\,x^3\,dx$$

$$\left[\frac{x^3}{3}\right]_0^h \bar{x} = \left[\frac{x^4}{4}\right]_0^h$$

$$\bar{x} = \frac{3}{4}\,h$$

This confirms the result of question 2, Exercise 1.

Example 2

A uniform solid cone and hemisphere, made of the same material, are joined at their circular faces. Find the centre of mass of the combined solid if the height of the cone is h metres and the circular faces are each of radius r metres.

The position of the centre of mass of the hemisphere is $\dfrac{3}{8}\,r$ metres from the plane face.

This is found by using calculus in a similar way to that used for the cone.

Solution

> **Set up a model**

The mass of the cone is $\dfrac{1}{3}\,\pi\,r^2 h\,\rho$ where ρ is the mass per unit volume. Its centre of mass is $\dfrac{3}{4}\,h$ from the vertex.

The mass of the hemisphere is $\dfrac{2}{3}\,\pi\,r^3\,\rho$ and the centre of mass is $\dfrac{3}{8}\,r$ from the plane face.

The x-coordinate of the centre of mass of the composite body is $\bar{x}$.

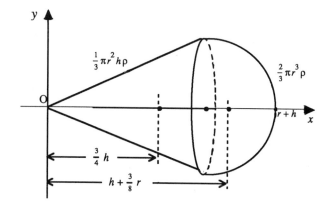

$$\left(\tfrac{1}{3}\pi r^2 h \rho + \tfrac{2}{3}\pi r^3 \rho\right)\bar{x} = \tfrac{1}{3}\pi r^2 h \rho\left(\tfrac{3}{4}h\right) + \tfrac{2}{3}\pi r^3 \rho\left(h + \tfrac{3}{8}r\right)$$

$$(h + 2r)\,\bar{x} = \tfrac{3}{4}h^2 + \tfrac{r}{4}\,(8h + 3r)$$

The distance in metres of the centre of mass of the solid from the vertex of the cone is

$$\frac{3h^2 + 8rh + 3r^2}{4(h + 2r)}$$

It lies on the axis of symmetry.

Exercise 2

1. Show that the centre of mass of a uniform solid hemisphere of radius r is $\tfrac{3}{8}r$ along the axis of symmetry from the plane circular face.

2. Find the positions of the centres of mass of the following composite bodies formed by combinations of a uniform solid cone, height h, base radius r; a uniform solid circular cylinder, height h, base radius r; and a uniform solid hemisphere of radius r. The bodies are all made of the same material.

    (a) The cone and cylinder joined at their circular faces.

    (b) The cylinder and the hemisphere joined at their circular faces.

3. A 'wobbly man' is made by joining two uniform solid shapes, a cone and hemisphere, by their circular faces. Find the condition on the height of the cone in terms of the radius of their joint circular faces if the wobbly man is always to return to an upright position when placed with any point of the hemisphere on a horizontal surface.

4. At the start of the evening a full can of cola stands on the table. Later it stands empty on the table. The centre of mass is in the same place in each case. Where has it been in between times, when the can was partially full? How low down the can did it go?

After working through this chapter you should:

1. know the conditions under which toppling will occur and be able to solve simple problems involving sliding or toppling;

2. understand the difference between the centre of mass and the centre of gravity;

3. know how to use calculus to calculate the positions of the centres of mass of various basic uniform rigid bodies;

4. be able to calculate the positions of the centres of mass of combinations of such rigid bodies.

Toppling

A hollow circular cylinder rests with one of its circular faces on a rough plane. The plane is horizontal to start with and is then slowly tilted. What will happen?

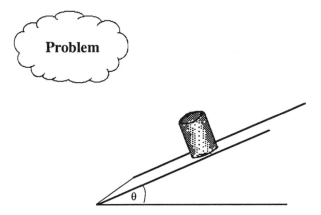

Problem

1.   List the variables which might affect what happens.

2.   Investigate practically using hollow cylinders. You can make these from the inside of a kitchen roll which can be cut to various lengths.

3.   Model the situation mathematically and interpret your findings.

1. A uniform cube of side 10 cm and mass 100 grams is pushed horizontally across a table-top with a force of P newtons. The line of action of the force passes through a point 8 cm above the base of the cube. The coefficient of friction betwen the cube and the table is 0.4. Will the cube topple or slide as P increases from zero?

2. A uniform cylinder of height $2h$ metres and radius r metres is placed on a rough board which is gradually tilted. Find a condition on μ (the coefficient of friction between the cylinder and the board) if the cylinder slides before it topples.

3. A woman is pushing a uniform cubical packing case of edge 1.5 metres and mass 10 kg

    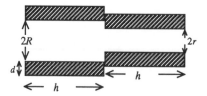

    towards the rear of a lorry. She pushes with a force of 30 newtons horizontally at the top of the packing case so that it slides.

    How much of the case can overhang the end of the lorry before it starts to topple?

4. Find the position of the centre of mass of a body formed by removing the top third of a hollow cone as shown.

    (The centre of mass of a hollow cone of base radius r metres and height d metres is $\frac{1}{3}d$ metres from the base.)

    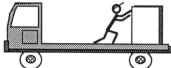

5. A connector for two pipes of different diameters is cast in the form of two hollow cylinders joined symmetrically end to end as shown.

    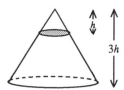

    If their internal diameters are $2r$ and $2R$ and they are both of thickness d and length h, find the position of the centre of mass of the connector. (All measurements are in metres.)

3 *Rotation and energy*

3.1 Rotational energy

A man walks up to a stationary revolving door and pushes it. It starts to revolve and he walks through.

- Does the man do work when he pushes the door?
- Does it matter where he pushes?
- Does the door have any energy as it rotates?

Experience and theory suggest that he will need to do work in order to start the door rotating. You know that he needs to apply a force to the push bar and the point of application of his force, i.e. the bar, will move as he pushes. The distance his hands move will be $r\,\theta$ metres, where r metres is the distance of his hands from the pivot and θ radians is the angle through which the door has turned.

If he applies a force of magnitude F newtons, then, since work done = force x distance

$$\text{work done} = F\,r\,\theta \text{ joules}$$

> **Why does this formula imply that it is easier to push on the outside edge of the door?**

 TASKSHEET 1 – *Rotating bodies*

35

Consider a heavy rod of length $2a$ metres spinning about its centre of mass with an angular speed of ω rad s^{-1}.

Suppose the rod is modelled as a particle at the rod's centre of mass. The particle does not move so it does not have any kinetic energy.

However, if the rod is modelled as a set of small particles, then each of those particles (except the particle at the centre) is moving.

> **Find the kinetic energy of the rotating rod, modelling it as a set of small particles.**

You will have seen that the kinetic energy of the rod is $\frac{1}{2}\left(\sum mr^2\right)\omega^2$ joules.

The quantity $\sum mr^2$ is called the **moment of inertia** of the rod and is usually represented by I.

> **The rotational kinetic energy of any body spinning about a fixed axis with angular speed ω rad s^{-1} is given by:**
>
> $$\text{KE} = \frac{1}{2}\left(\sum mr^2\right)\omega^2 = \frac{1}{2}I\omega^2 \text{ joules}$$

When working through Tasksheet 1 you will have noticed that for a rod of given mass its moment of inertia depends upon the way in which that mass is distributed. In practice, moments of inertia are usually calculated assuming uniform distribution of mass. Methods of evaluating moments of inertia are considered in the next section.

The similarity between the formulas $\frac{1}{2}I\omega^2$ and $\frac{1}{2}Mv^2$ for kinetic energy of rotational and linear motion is striking. Moreover, the energy principle:

> **work done by the resultant force = change in kinetic energy**

applies to rotational as well as to linear motion.

Example 1

A turntable is rotating at an angular speed of 45 r.p.m. Its moment of inertia about the axis of rotation is 0.2 kg m².

(a)   What is its rotational kinetic energy?

(b)   If the turntable has radius 16 cm and is accelerated from rest by a force of 1 newton acting on the rim, how many revolutions does it take to reach 45 r.p.m.?

Solution

(a)   Angular speed $= 45 \times 2\pi \div 60$ rad s^{-1} $= 1.5\pi$ rad s^{-1}
Rotational KE $= \frac{1}{2}I\omega^2 = 0.1 \times (1.5\pi)^2 = 0.225 \pi^2$ joules

(b)   Assuming there are no energy losses as the turntable turns through θ radians,

work done from rest $= F r \theta = 0.16 \theta$

work done = KE gained, so $0.16 \theta = 0.225\pi^2 \Rightarrow \theta \approx 13.88$

The number of revolutions is 2.2 (to 2 s.f.).

Exercise 1

1.   A turntable is rotating at 78 r.p.m. Its moment of inertia about the axis of rotation is 0.1 kg m². What is its rotational kinetic energy?

2.   The moment of inertia of a bicycle wheel about the axis is 0.05 kg m². Assuming the axis is smooth, what work must be done to make it spin at 40 rad s^{-1} from rest?

3.   A rotating disc loses 1000 joules of rotational kinetic energy when its angular speed drops from 10 rad s^{-1} to 5 rad s^{-1}. What is its moment of inertia about the axis of rotation?

4.   A light rod of length 2 metres has a particle of mass 10 grams at each end. The rod is spinning about an axis through its centre, perpendicular to the plane of the rod, at an angular speed of 4 rad s^{-1}. Find the rotational kinetic energy of the system.

5.   A light rod of length d metres has n particles, each of mass $\frac{m}{n}$ kilograms distributed equally along its length (with one at each end). The rod is spinning about an axis through one end, perpendicular to the plane of the rod, at an angular speed of ω rad s^{-1}. Find the kinetic energy of the rod if :

(a) $n = 3$;   (b) $n = 5$;   (c) $n = 101$.

6.   A large cotton reel of radius 5 cm is free to rotate on a smooth vertical spindle. The cotton is pulled with a constant force of 2 newtons. The moment of inertia of the reel is 0.0003 kg m² and the reel starts from rest. After one revolution, find:

(a)   the kinetic energy of the reel;   (b)   the angular speed of the reel.

3.2   Moment of inertia

In the previous section you saw that a body rotating around a fixed axis has a rotational inertia called its **moment of inertia**. This quantity, I, depends upon the distribution of the mass of the body about the axis.

$$I = \Sigma \, mr^2$$

The calculation of the moment of inertia of a rigid body about a fixed axis can be done in one of two ways:

(a) by simple summation, for a body made up from a finite number of particles;

(b) by integration, for a solid body whose mass is distributed over the body.

These methods are illustrated in the following examples.

Example 2

Two rods of negligible mass and each of length $2a$ metres are fixed together at their common mid-point O to form a cross as shown. Particles A, B, C and D of mass m, $2m$, $3m$ and $4m$ kilograms respectively are fixed to the ends of the rods.

Find the moment of inertia of the body:

(a) about an axis perpendicular to the plane ABCD through O;

(b) about an axis along AB;

(c) about an axis along AC.

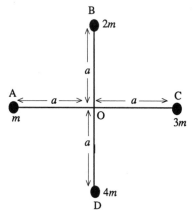

Solution

(a) A is a distance a from the pivot at O, so the moment of inertia of the particle at A is ma^2. Similarly, the moments of inertia of particles B, C, and D are $2ma^2$, $3ma^2$ and $4ma^2$.

Thus, the moment of inertia of the whole body about an axis perpendicular to the plane ABCD through O is

$$ma^2 + 2ma^2 + 3ma^2 + 4ma^2 \; = \; 10ma^2 \; \text{kg m}^2$$

(b) A lies on AB, so the moment of inertia of A about AB is zero.
Similarly, the moment of inertia of B about AB is zero.
C is a distance $a \sqrt{2}$ from AB so the moment of inertia of C about AB is $3m \, (a \, \sqrt{2})^2 \; = \; 6ma^2$.
D is a distance $a \sqrt{2}$ from AB so the moment of inertia of D about AB is $4m \, (a \, \sqrt{2})^2 \; = \; 8ma^2$.
The total moment of inertia about AB is $14ma^2$ kg m^2.

(c) A lies on AC, so the moment of inertia of A about AC is zero.
Similarly, the moment of inertia of C about AC is zero.
B is a distance a from AC, so the moment of inertia of B about AC is $2ma^2$.
D is a distance a from AC, so the moment of inertia of D about AC is $4ma^2$.
The total moment of inertia of the system about AC is $6ma^2$ kg m^2.

Example 3

Find the moment of inertia of a uniform rod of length $2a$ metres and mass per unit length ρ kilograms:

(a)   about an axis though its centre of gravity perpendicular to the rod;

(b)   about an axis through one end of the rod perpendicular to the rod;

(c)   about an axis parallel to the rod a distance h metres away.

Solution

The mass M of the rod is $2\rho a$ kilograms.

(a)   The mass of an element of length dx is $\rho\, dx$.

If the element is a distance x from the axis, then the moment of inertia about the axis is $\rho\, dx\, x^2$. For the whole rod you need to sum these quantities.

$$\text{Moment of inertia} = \Sigma \rho\, x^2\, dx$$

$$= \int_{-a}^{a} x^2 \rho\, dx$$

$$= \left[\tfrac{1}{3} \rho x^3 \right]_{-a}^{a}$$

$$= \tfrac{2}{3} \rho a^3$$

$$= \tfrac{1}{3} Ma^2 \text{ kg m}^2$$

(b)   Let the moment of inertia of the rod about an axis through one end be I.

$$I = \int_{0}^{2a} x^2 \rho\, dx$$

$$= \left[\tfrac{1}{3} \rho x^3 \right]_{0}^{2a}$$

$$= \tfrac{8}{3} \rho a^3$$

$$= \tfrac{4}{3} Ma^2 \text{ kg m}^2$$

39

(c)   Every element is a distance h from the axis.

The moment of inertia of each element about the axis is $\rho \, dx \, h^2$.

Axis of rotation

Moment of inertia of whole rod $= \int_0^{2a} h^2 \rho \, dx = Mh^2 \text{ kg m}^2$

You can see that there is no unique value for the moment of inertia of a body. It depends upon the position of the body relative to the axis of rotation.

> The moment of inertia of a rigid body about an axis is $\sum mr^2$ where m is the mass of a typical element of the body and r is the perpendicular distance of the element from the axis.
>
> The moment of inertia of a composite body about an axis is equal to the sums of the moments of inertia of the components about the axis.

The table below gives the moments of inertia of several simple bodies about various axes. Unless specifically asked to derive these results, you may quote them without proof.

Uniform body of mass M	Axis	Moment of inertia
Rod of length $2a$	Through centre, perpendicular to rod	$\frac{1}{3} Ma^2$
	Through end, perpendicular to rod	$\frac{4}{3} Ma^2$
Ring of radius r	Through centre, perpendicular to plane of ring	Mr^2
	Along diameter	$\frac{1}{2} Mr^2$
Disc of radius r	Through centre, perpendicular to disc	$\frac{1}{2} Mr^2$
	Along diameter	$\frac{1}{4} Mr^2$
Solid sphere of radius r	Through centre	$\frac{2}{5} Mr^2$
Hollow sphere of radius r	Through centre	$\frac{2}{3} Mr^2$
Square lamina of side $2a$	Along one side	$\frac{4}{3} Ma^2$
	Through centre, perpendicular to plane	$\frac{2}{3} Ma^2$
	Through centre, in the plane of the lamina	$\frac{1}{3} Ma^2$

Exercise 2

1. Find the moment of inertia of a system of three particles, each of mass 1 kg and fixed at the vertices of a light equilateral triangle of side 1 metre, about an axis:

    (a)   through one vertex parallel to the opposite side;

    (b)   through one vertex perpendicular to the plane of the triangle;

    (c)   along one side of the triangle.

2. Find the moment of inertia of a thin hollow cylinder of mass M kilograms, and radius r metres, about the axis of the cylinder.

3. Find the moment of inertia of a uniform rod of length 10 cm and mass 10 grams about an axis perpendicular to the rod and 3 cm from the centre of the rod:

    (a)   from first principles;

    (b)   by considering the rod as two rods joined end to end.

4. Find the moment of inertia of a solid uniform sphere of mass 5 kg and radius 20 cm about an axis through the centre of the sphere.

5. A body is made from two uniform rods, each of length $2l$ metres and mass M kilograms, fixed together to form an L shape. Find its moment of inertia about an axis perpendicular to the plane of the shape through the point at which they join.

3.3   Conservation of mechanical energy

In *Modelling with circular motion* you learnt that if no external work is done on a particle, other than by gravity, then the total mechanical energy of the particle remains constant.

This principle applies equally to rotating rigid bodies. The sum of potential and kinetic energy remains constant as long as no work is done other than by gravity. In this case, if the body is rotating round a fixed axis or pivot then there must be no resistance to rotation due to friction at the pivot. The body is then said to be **rotating freely** about the pivot.

There is nearly always a force acting on the body due to the pivot but if the body rotates freely and the pivot is stationary this force will do no work.

The potential energy of a particle of mass M kilograms at a height of h metres above the ground is Mgh joules relative to the ground. What is the potential energy of a rigid body of equal mass?

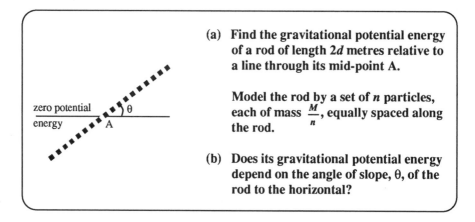

(a) **Find the gravitational potential energy of a rod of length 2d metres relative to a line through its mid-point A.**

Model the rod by a set of n particles, each of mass $\dfrac{M}{n}$, equally spaced along the rod.

(b) **Does its gravitational potential energy depend on the angle of slope, θ, of the rod to the horizontal?**

The potential energy of a rigid body is easy to calculate using the following result.

> **The potential energy of a rigid body is equal to that of a particle of the same mass situated at the centre of gravity of the body.**

You will now be able to use the principle of conservation of mechanical energy for a rotating body.

Example 4

A gymnast balances on her hands on a high bar. She then rotates freely
about the bar until she is hanging vertically below it.

(a) Assuming that she is modelled as a uniform rod, if the distance
     between her centre of gravity and her hands is 1 metre and her
     mass is 60 kg, estimate her moment of inertia about the bar and
     hence estimate her angular speed when she reaches her lowest point.

(b) What would your answer be if you had modelled the gymnast as a
     light rod with a particle of mass 60 kg one metre from the pivot?

Solution

(a) | Set up a model |

Assume that the gymnast can be modelled as a uniform heavy rod of length
2 metres and mass 60 kg rotating freely about an axis 1 metre from her centre of
gravity. Assume that she has an angular speed of ω when she reaches the bottom
of her swing.

| Analyse the problem |

Her moment of inertia about the bar is $\frac{4}{3}$ x 60 x 1^2 = 80 kg m^2.

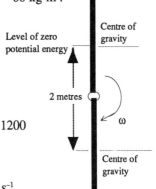

Initial KE = 0   Initial PE = 0

Final KE = $\frac{1}{2} I \omega^2$ = 40 ω^2

Final PE = mgh = – 60 x 10 x 2 = – 1200 joules

But mechanical energy is conserved, so 0 = 40 ω^2 – 1200

$$\omega^2 = \frac{1200}{40}$$

$$\omega = 5.48 \text{ rad s}^{-1}$$

(b) Assume the gymnast can be modelled as a particle of mass 60 kg at the end of a
     light rod of length 1 metre.

Initial PE = 0   Initial KE = 0

Final PE = mgh = – 1200 joules

Final KE = $\frac{1}{2} mv^2 = \frac{1}{2} mr^2 \omega^2$ = 30 ω^2

But energy is conserved, so 30 ω^2 = 1200

$$\omega = 6.32 \text{ rad s}^{-1}$$

The particle model has given a higher estimate of angular speed than the rigid body model because it has ignored the motion of the athlete's body relative to its centre of mass.

TASKSHEET 2 – *Finding moments of inertia*

Exercise 3

1. A girl balances a pencil vertically on its point on a table. The pencil then topples without sliding. Find its angular speed as it hits the table, assuming that it may be modelled as a uniform rod of length 15 cm.

2. A barrier at a car park is in the form of a uniform pole of mass 20 kg and length 5 metres, freely pivoted about a point 1 metre from its end. When it is vertical, it is displaced slightly by a gust of wind. Estimate its angular speed as it reaches the horizontal.

3. A uniform body of mass 2 kg is pivoted a distance 20 cm from its centre of gravity. It swings under gravity at exactly the same angular speed as a particle of equal mass on the end of a light string of length 30 cm. What is the moment of inertia of the body?

4. A tree of height 50 metres and mass 2 tonnes is to be cut down.

   (a) Assuming it can be modelled as a uniform rod freely rotating about a pivot at the base, find its angular speed as it hits the ground.

   (b) What is the speed of the top of the tree as it hits the ground?

   (c) Discuss why your answer is likely to be either an underestimate or an overestimate.

   Validate your answer by making cardboard models of a pine tree and an oak tree, with the same mass. Stand them side by side on a table and release them together. Which hits the table first?

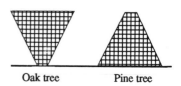

   Oak tree   Pine tree

5. A boy is swinging on the end of a heavy rope. His speed when at the bottom of his swing is 6 ms⁻¹. The rope has mass 20 kg and length 10 metres and the boy can be modelled as a heavy particle of mass 25 kg hanging at the bottom. Find the greatest angle the rope makes with the vertical.

3.4   Parallel axis theorem

In Section 3.2, you saw that the moment of inertia of a rod is different for different axes of rotation. If the moment of inertia about an axis through the centre of mass is known, then its moment of inertia about any parallel axis can be calculated.

The parallel axis theorem states:

If the moment of inertia of a body of mass M kilograms about a fixed axis through its centre of mass is I_G then its moment of inertia about a parallel axis a distance d metres from this fixed axis is given by
$$I_D = I_G + Md^2.$$

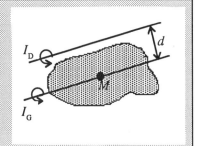

Test this theorem using the various moments of inertia of a rod calculated in Example 3.

The theorem appears to hold in the cases that you have tested. However, to prove that it holds in all cases requires a general proof.

Consider a body of mass M which has a moment of inertia I_G about an axis GG_1 through its centre of mass G.

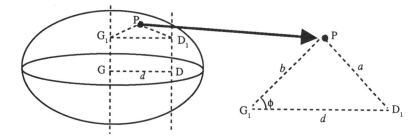

If m is the mass of a typical particle and b is its distance from GG_1, then $I_G = \Sigma mb^2$.

Let a parallel axis DD_1 be a distance d from the axis GG_1.
The moment of inertia of the body about DD_1 is Σma^2, where $a^2 = b^2 + d^2 - 2bd \cos \phi$.

So the moment of inertia about DD_1 is $\Sigma mb^2 + d^2 \Sigma m - 2d \Sigma mb \cos \phi$

$$\Rightarrow I_D = I_G + d^2 M - 2d \Sigma mb \cos \phi$$

Use the definition of the centre of mass to explain why $\Sigma mb \cos \phi = 0$.

Therefore, $I_D = I_G + Md^2$

Example 5

Use the parallel axis theorem to find the moment of inertia of a uniform rod of length $4d$ metres and mass M kg about an axis perpendicular to the rod passing through a point on the rod a distance d metres from the mid point.

Solution

The moment of inertia of the rod about an axis through its centre of gravity is $\frac{1}{3} M (2d)^2 = \frac{4}{3} M d^2$.

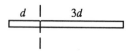

By the parallel axis theorem, the moment of inertia about the new axis is $\frac{4}{3} M d^2 + M d^2 = \frac{7}{3} M d^2$.

Exercise 4

1. Find the moment of inertia of a hollow sphere of mass 10 kg and radius 15 cm about an axis 1 metre from its centre.

2. Find the moment of inertia of a solid sphere of the same mass and radius about an axis 1 metre from its centre.

3. Find the moment of inertia of a disc of mass 1 kg and radius 50 cm about an axis perpendicular to the disc through a point on the circumference of the disc.

4. A drum majorette's baton is made from two solid spheres, each of radius 5 cm and mass 100 grams, joined by a uniform rod of mass 100 grams and length 1 metre. Find the moment of inertia of the baton about an axis perpendicular to the rod:

    (a) through the mid-point of the rod;

    (b) through the centre of one of the spheres.

5. The pendulum of a grandfather clock is made from a rod of length 1 metre and mass 0.1 kg with a disc of radius 3 cm and mass 0.2 kg fixed to the rod a distance 80 cm from the axis of rotation through the end of the rod.

    (a) Find the moment of inertia about its axis of rotation.

    (b) How will the moment of inertia of the system change if you move the disc nearer the axis of rotation?

6. The moment of inertia of a solid cylinder of mass 12 kg about an axis 50 cm from its centre of gravity is 5.5 kg m². Find its moment of inertia about a parallel axis a distance 20 cm from its centre of gravity.

3.5   Perpendicular axes theorem

Another useful theorem on moments of inertia is the perpendicular axes theorem. This holds only for thin laminas, **not** for 3-dimensional bodies.

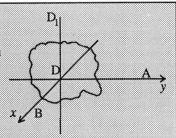

If the moment of inertia of a plane lamina about two perpendicular axes in the plane of the body are I_A and I_B respectively, then the moment of inertia of the body about an axis through the same point perpendicular to the lamina is $I_A + I_B$.

> Test this theorem using some of the moments of inertia given in the table in Section 3.2, for example those for the ring and those for the square.

Once again this test does not constitute a proof. It only tells you that the theorem may be true.

Consider a body of mass M kilograms which has a moment of inertia I_A about an axis DA in the plane of the lamina through a point. Let the moment of inertia of the body about a perpendicular axis DB also in the plane, be I_B. Let its moment of inertia about an axis DD_1 through D, perpendicular to the lamina, be I. You need to prove that $I = I_A + I_B$.

Let m kilograms be the mass of a typical particle, x metres its distance from the first axis, y metres its distance from the second axis and r metres its distance from the axis perpendicular to the lamina.

Then $I_A = \sum mx^2$ and $I_B = \sum my^2$

The moment of inertia of each particle about the axis perpendicular to the lamina is mr^2 where $r^2 = x^2 + y^2$.

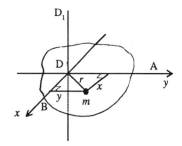

So $I = \sum mr^2 = \sum m(x^2 + y^2)$
$\quad = \sum mx^2 + \sum my^2$

$\Rightarrow I = I_A + I_B$

Example 6

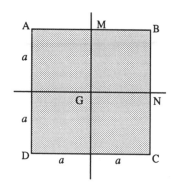

The moment of inertia about an axis parallel to one side through its centre of gravity, G, of a uniform square lamina ABCD of side $2a$ metres and mass M kg is $\frac{1}{3}Ma^2$.

Find the moment of inertia, I, of the lamina about an axis through G perpendicular to the plane ABCD and hence find the moment of inertia of the lamina about AC.

Solution

The moment of inertia of the lamina about GM is $\frac{1}{3}Ma^2$.
By symmetry, the moment of inertia of the lamina about GN is also $\frac{1}{3}Ma^2$.

Therefore $I = \frac{1}{3}Ma^2 + \frac{1}{3}Ma^2 = \frac{2}{3}Ma^2$

As the lamina is square, AC is perpendicular to BD and, by symmetry, the moment of inertia of the lamina is the same about each.

Hence $I = I_{AC} + I_{BD} = 2I_{AC}$ so $I_{AC} = \frac{1}{3}Ma^2$

Exercise 5

1. A rectangular lamina ABCD of mass M kg has sides AB $= a$ metres and BC $= b$ metres. Its moment of inertia about AD is $\frac{1}{3}Ma^2$. Find its moment of inertia about an axis perpendicular to ABCD through A.

2. A lamina of mass 3 kg is in the shape of a quadrant of a circle of radius 40 cm. Find its moment of inertia about one of its straight edges.

3. A circular metal washer has mass M kg, internal radius 1 metre and external radius 2 metres. Find its moment of inertia about an axis along a diameter. (The moment of inertia of a disc about a perpendicular axis through its centre is $\frac{1}{2}Ma^2$.)

4. A table tennis player balances the end of the handle of his bat on his finger. It starts to topple. Assume that the bat can be modelled as a circular disc of mass 30 grams and radius 8 cm on a rod of mass 30 grams and length 10 cm. Find its angular speed when it is horizontal if it rotates:

   (a) about an axis perpendicular to the face of the bat;

   (b) about an axis parallel to the face of the bat.

After working though this chapter you should:

1. know that the rotational kinetic energy of any body rotating about a fixed axis with angular speed ω rad s^{-1} is given by the formula $KE = \frac{1}{2} I \omega^2$, where I is the moment of inertia of the body about the axis;

2. know that the potential energy of a rigid body relative to a given position is equal to the potential energy of a particle of equal mass situated at the centre of gravity of the rigid body;

3. be able to find the moment of inertia, about a given axis, of a body composed of a finite number of particles;

4. be able to find the moment of inertia about a given axis of a simple lamina;

5. know that the moment of inertia of a composite body about an axis is equal to the sum of the moments of inertia of its component parts about that axis;

6. understand and be able to apply the parallel and perpendicular axes theorems;

7. know that if a body is rotating freely about a fixed axis then its mechanical energy is conserved.

Rotating bodies

You will need a ruler or strip of wood or plastic with a hole drilled in the centre, a large strip of Blu-Tack or Plasticine and a clampstand or nail fixed to the table so that the rod can rotate freely in a vertical plane.

1.   Use your finger to spin the rod at about 2 revolutions a second. How easy was it to start? Did your finger do any work?

2.   Stick a strip of Blu-Tack symmetrically at both sides of the pivot point as shown and repeat question 1.

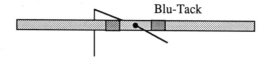

Blu-Tack

Did you need to do more work this time?

3.   Move the Blu-Tack further out towards the ends of the ruler and repeat. What happens now?

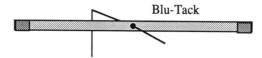

Blu-Tack

4.   How does the distribution of mass appear to affect what happens?

5.   Put as much Blu-Tack as possible along the ruler, making sure it still balances, and repeat the experiment.

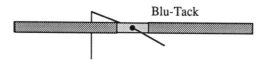

Blu-Tack

6.   When the rod is spinning, what can you say about its:

   (a)   linear motion;

   (b)   rotational motion;

   (c)   kinetic energy?

7.   Explain what happens if you model the rod as a single particle.

Finding moments of inertia

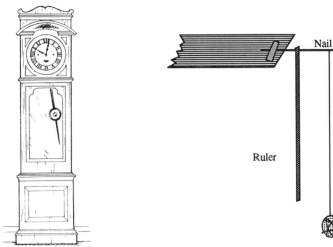

You will need a rod or ruler of known mass with a hole drilled in one end, a lump of Blu-Tack of the same mass as the ruler, a piece of string and a clampstand or nail fixed to the table so that the rod can rotate freely in a vertical plane.

1.   Tie the string round the nail and wind the other end round the Blu-Tack as shown, so that it is a little longer than the ruler. Hook the ruler on the nail.

2.   Set them swinging together.

3.   Adjust the length of the string so that the two swing together at the same rate. Measure the length of the string and the length of the rod.

4.   What can you say about the angular speeds of the two objects when they are swinging together?

5.   Start the two swinging from a fixed angle θ with the downward vertical. Let their angular speed when the rod and string are vertical be ω. Modelling the Blu-Tack as a particle on the end of a light string, write down the energy equations for both the rod and string, using I for the moment of inertia of the rod about the pivot.

6.   Use these equations to obtain a numerical value for I.

7.   Validate your answer by using the formula for the moment of inertia of a rod through an axis at one end.

8.   Use this method to find the moment of inertia about the pivot of a cardboard cutout of a gymnast when swinging round a horizontal bar. What happens if the gymnast changes his stance?

Tutorial sheet

1. A uniform rod of length 20 cm and mass 300 grams is rotating about a point 5 cm from one end. Its speed of rotation is 20 rad s^{-1}. Find the kinetic energy of the rod.

2. A swingboat can be modelled as two uniform rods, AB and CD, each 12 m long as shown. AB has mass 200 kg and CD has mass 600 kg.

   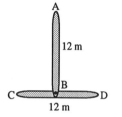

   (a) Find the moment of inertia of the boat about an axis through A, perpendicular to AB.

   (b) Assuming that the boat can rotate freely about A, find the maximum height B can reach if it has an angular speed of 0.5 rad s^{-1} in the position shown.

   (c) A different model is set up assuming that the boat is a particle of mass 800 kg at B suspended by a light rod from A. Find the maximum height B could reach using this model.

3. A tall factory chimney has mass 3000 kg, height 20 metres and a square base of side 2 metres. It is demolished by removing the supports from one side so that it rotates about AB. What is the speed of the top of the chimney as it hits the ground:

   (a) if the chimney is modelled as a rod of length 20 metres;

   (b) if the chimney is modelled as a rectangular lamina 2 metres by 20 metres, perpendicular to AB?

4 *Rotation and angular acceleration*

4.1 Moment of momentum – angular momentum

A penny on a turntable may be modelled as a particle of mass m travelling with angular speed ω in a circle of radius r anticlockwise about an axis.

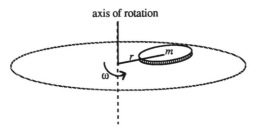

Its momentum is mv or $mr\omega$ parallel to the velocity.

The moment of this momentum about the axis of rotation is defined as the product of the magnitude of the momentum and the distance of the particle from the axis of rotation: rmv or $mr^2\omega$. This is called the **angular momentum** of the particle about the axis of rotation.

> **The angular momentum (or moment of momentum) of a particle of mass m kg about an axis is $mr^2\omega$, where r is its distance in metres from the axis and ω is the angular speed in rad s^{-1}.**
>
> **Angular momentum is measured in kg m^2 s^{-1}.**

The concept of angular momentum can be extended from a particle to a rigid body.

Consider a body rotating about an axis with angular speed ω rad s^{-1}.

The body can be modelled by a collection of particles of mass m kg and distance r metres from the axis of rotation.

Each particle has a moment of momentum. These can be summed to give the total angular momentum.

$$
\begin{aligned}
\text{Angular momentum} &= \sum m r^2 \omega \\
&= \left(\sum m r^2\right) \omega \\
&= I\omega
\end{aligned}
$$

where I is the moment of inertia of the body about the axis of rotation.

You may notice the similarity between the expressions for linear momentum, Mv and angular momentum $I\omega$.

> **The angular momentum of a body rotating with angular**
> **speed ω rad s^{-1} about an axis is $I\omega$ kg m^2 s^{-1}, where I is the**
> **moment of inertia of the body about the axis of rotation.**

A potter drops a large lump of clay onto the centre of a freely spinning potter's wheel. What do you think happens to the angular speed of the wheel?

Does your answer depend on:

(a) **the mass of the clay;**

(b) **the shape of the clay?**

In *Newton's laws of motion* you saw that for a system of particles the total linear momentum of the system is conserved if no external forces act.

Similarly, unless some external forces exert a torque on the system, the total angular momentum of the system is conserved. This is called the **principle of conservation of angular momentum**.

Example 1

A girl of mass 45 kg is standing on a roundabout of radius 4 metres which is spinning freely about the central axis. She starts at a distance of 2 metres from the central axis. The moment of inertia of the roundabout about the axis is 200 kg m^2 and it is spinning with an angular speed of 3 rad s^{-1}.

Describe the motion of the roundabout if she:

(a)   walks to the centre of the roundabout;

(b)   walks to the edge of the roundabout.

Solution

Set up a model

Assume that the girl can be modelled as a particle of mass 45 kg.

Assume that there is no torque acting on the axis of rotation of the roundabout.

(a)   Initial angular momentum $= 45 \times 2^2 \times 3 + 200 \times 3 = 1140$ kg m^2 s^{-1}

Final angular momentum $= 45 \times 0 \times \omega + 200 \times \omega = 200\omega$

Angular momentum is conserved, so $200\omega = 1140$
$$\Rightarrow \omega = 5.7 \text{ rad s}^{-1}$$

(b)   If she now walks to the outside of the roundabout,

final angular momentum $= 45 \times 4^2 \times \omega + 200 \times \omega = 920\omega$

Angular momentum is conserved, so $920\omega = 1140$
$$\Rightarrow \omega = 1.24 \text{ rad s}^{-1}$$

Interpret /Validate

As the girl walks towards the centre of the roundabout, the moment of inertia of the system decreases and the angular speed increases. As she walks outwards, the moment of inertia increases and the angular speed decreases. In both cases the angular momentum remains constant.

You could validate this yourself in a playground.

Exercise 1

1.   A skater spins freely round at 4 rad s^{-1} with his arms outstretched. His moment of inertia about his axis of spin in this position is I kg m^2. He pulls in his arms so that his new moment of inertia about the axis of spin is $\frac{3}{4}I$ kg m^2. What is his new angular speed? How much work was done to bring his arms in to his side?

2.   An icing turntable (with a rough surface), of moment of inertia 4 kg m^2 about the axis of spin and angular speed 10 rad s^{-1}, is spinning freely. A Christmas cake of identical moment of inertia about the same axis is dropped onto the turntable.

    (a)   What is the angular speed of the new system?

    (b)   What would happen if the table was completely smooth?

3.   A stack of records drops onto the turntable of an old record player that is rotating freely at 78 r.p.m. with the motor disconnected. The turntable has moment of inertia 0.1 kg m^2 about the axis of spin and each record has moment of inertia of 0.02 kg m^2 about an axis through its centre. Plot a graph to show the angular speed of the turntable against the number of records dropped on it.

4.2 Acceleration of a particle moving in a circle

In *Modelling with circular motion* you found that the acceleration of a particle P, moving in a circle of radius r, has components $r\ddot{\theta}$ tangentially and $r\dot{\theta}^2$ towards the centre.

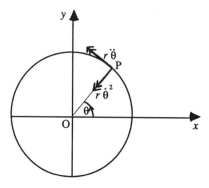

(a) What is meant by $\ddot{\theta}$ and $\dot{\theta}$?

(b) Write down as a column vector the position vector of P relative to O.

(c) Confirm by differentiation that the acceleration of P has components $r\dot{\theta}^2$ in the direction $\overrightarrow{PO}$ and $r\ddot{\theta}$ tangentially in the direction of increasing θ.

TASKSHEET 1 – *The windscreen wiper*

Example 2

Suppose a particle moves in a circle of radius 4 metres and its angular displacement in radians at time t seconds is given by $\theta = 1 - \cos t$, where θ is the angle from the x-axis as shown.

Find the velocity and acceleration of P at time t.

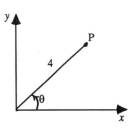

Solution

$\theta = 1 - \cos t \Rightarrow \dot{\theta} = \sin t$ and $\ddot{\theta} = \cos t$

Velocity $= r\dot{\theta} = 4 \sin t$ ms^{-1} tangentially

Its acceleration has components $r\dot{\theta}^2 = 4 \sin^2 t$ ms^{-2} towards the centre

and $r\ddot{\theta} = 4 \cos t$ ms^{-2} tangentially.

Velocity

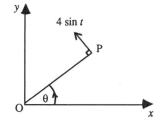

Acceleration

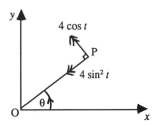

Example 3

A particle A moves in a circle of radius 2 metres.

If $\theta = t^2$ after time t seconds, calculate the speed and the components of the acceleration of A after 2 seconds.

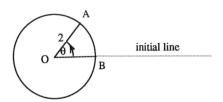

Solution

$\theta = t^2 \Rightarrow \dot{\theta} = 2t$ and $\ddot{\theta} = 2$

Speed $= r\dot{\theta} = 2 \times 2t = 4t$

When $t = 2$, the speed of A $= 8$ ms^{-1}.

Acceleration is $r\dot\theta^2 = 2 \times (2t)^2 = 8t^2$ ms^{-2} towards the centre

and $r\ddot\theta = 2 \times 2 = 4$ ms^{-2} tangentially.

When $t = 2$, the components of the acceleration are 32 ms^{-2} radially inwards and 4 ms^{-2} tangentially.

Exercise 2

1. A string carrying a heavy weight unwinds from a pulley, centre O and radius 0.1 metres.

    A point P, on the rim of the pulley moves so that OP makes an angle of θ radians with the horizontal, where $\theta = 3t^2$.

    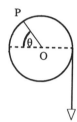

    Calculate the radial and tangential components of acceleration for P when $t = 1$ and when $t = 3$.
    Hence state the acceleration of the heavy weight.

2. A particle P performs a circle of radius 5 metres as shown.

    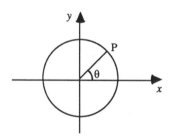

    At time t seconds, the angle θ radians is given by $\theta = 1 + 3 \sin t$. Find P's velocity and acceleration after two seconds. What is the angle between the velocity and the acceleration at that time?

3. A motor-cyclist crosses a hump-backed bridge which forms an arc of a vertical circle of radius 15 m. At the top of the hump he is travelling at 10 ms^{-1} and increasing speed at 2 ms^{-2}. Find the magnitude and direction of his acceleration at that instant.

4. A particle, P, travels in a circle of constant radius r.

    (a) Use $v = r\dot\theta$ to check that the tangential component of the acceleration is the rate of change of speed. Hence re-write the acceleration components in terms of the linear speed v instead of the angular speed $\dot\theta$.

    (b) What can be said about the speed if the acceleration is wholly radial?

    (c) Discuss the variation in the direction of the resultant acceleration of a pendulum bob as it swings in a vertical plane.

4.3   The equation for rotational motion

Consider a ruler fixed at one end and oscillating freely in a vertical plane.

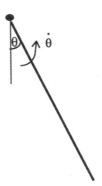

You know that energy is conserved, and in the last chapter you treated situations like this by writing down the energy equation involving the angular speed $\dot\theta$. But suppose that the pivot is rough so that there is a loss of energy. The energy equation then no longer applies. For a particle, Newton's second law is valid whether energy is lost or not. There is a corresponding equation for a rigid body that is rotating – an equation that is valid whether or not energy is lost.

In this section, the equation for rotational motion will be derived for the case of a body rotating about a fixed axis, such as a drawbridge, where there may be a loss of energy due to the frictional forces at the axis.

Problem

Find the equation for rotational motion of a drawbridge as it is lowered.

Set up a model

Modelling the bridge as a heavy rod of mass M kg as in the diagram:

OA is the drawbridge pivoted at O.
G is the centre of gravity of the
bridge, which need not be at the centre of
the rod. S and T are forces acting on the
bridge, and C is a torque acting at O.

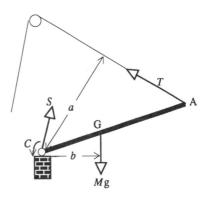

What do the variables S, T and C represent in the model?

Model the bridge as a collection of discrete particles and use Newton's second law for each particle. Since the bridge is rotating, it seems reasonable to consider the moments of the forces acting on the particles about the axis of rotation through O.

Consider the motion of one particle P of mass m as shown.

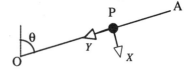

P is describing a circle, centre O. Suppose the forces acting on P are represented completely by the two components X and Y as shown.

These components will include the weight mg of the particle, and any internal forces due to its proximity to other particles. If P is at the end A, then the components X and Y will, in addition, include a part of the external force T due to the tension in the cables.

Let $OP = r$.

The acceleration of P is $r\dot\theta^2$ along PO and $r\ddot\theta$ perpendicular to OP in the direction of increasing θ.

Thus, using Newton's second law for P, $\quad mr\dot\theta^2 = Y$

$$mr\ddot\theta = X$$

Taking moments clockwise about the axis at O,

the total moment of all the forces acting on P $= Xr + Y \times 0 = Xr$
$$= mr^2\ddot\theta$$

The drawbridge is modelled as a large collection of such particles, so summing over all the particles gives:

$$\sum (Xr) = \sum (mr^2\ddot\theta) = \ddot\theta \sum (mr^2) = I\ddot\theta$$

Note that $\ddot\theta$ is the same for all the particles and $\sum (mr^2)$ is the moment of inertia I of the drawbridge about the axis through O.

$\sum(Xr) = \sum$ (moments of the external forces) $+ \sum$ (moments of the internal forces)

The internal forces are in pairs of equal magnitude and opposite direction because of Newton's third law, so the sum of their moments is zero. Hence

$$\sum (Fr) = I\ddot\theta$$

where $\sum(Fr)$ is the sum of the moments of the external forces about the axis.

The equation for the rotating drawbridge is

$$I\ddot{\theta} = \Sigma\,(Fr) = Mgb - Ta - C$$

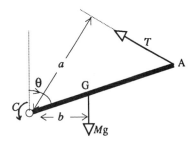

> **For a rigid body rotating about a fixed axis, the equation of rotational motion is given by:**
>
> $$\Sigma\,(Fr) = I\,\ddot{\theta}$$
>
> **where I is the moment of inertia of the body about the axis of rotation and ΣFr is the sum of the moments of all the external forces about the same axis in the direction of increasing θ.**

Example 4

The moment of inertia of a water-wheel about its axis is 30 kg m². When it is stationary, a constant couple of magnitude 45 Nm is applied to it.

Calculate its angular speed after 3 seconds and its kinetic energy at time t. Assume that the water-wheel rotates freely.

Solution

Using the equation of rotational motion, $I\ddot{\theta} = \Sigma\,(Fr)$

$$30\ddot{\theta} = 45 \Rightarrow \ddot{\theta} = 1.5$$

Integrating with respect to time, $\dot{\theta} = 1.5t + \text{constant}$

When $t = 0$, $\dot{\theta} = 0$, and so $\dot{\theta} = 1.5t$

When $t = 3$, $\dot{\theta} = 4.5$

Kinetic energy $= \frac{1}{2}I\omega^2 = \frac{1}{2} \times 30\,(1.5t)^2 = 33.75t^2$

The angular speed of the wheel after 3 seconds is 4.5 rad s⁻¹ and its kinetic energy at time t is $33.75t^2$ joules.

TASKSHEET 2 – *Flywheels*

Example 5

A heavy pulley of radius *r* metres and mass 4*m* kg has a light string hanging over it, the ends of which are attached to masses A and B, of *m* and 3*m* kg respectively.

Assuming that the pulley turns freely and that the string does not slip, find the acceleration of the masses.

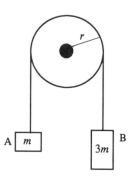

Solution

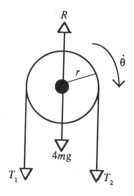

The diagram shows the forces acting on the pulley If the pulley turns freely, there will be no frictional couple opposing its motion. The forces acting on the pulley due to the masses A and B are T_1 and T_2.

Using $I\ddot{\theta} = \Sigma (Fr)$ and taking moments about the axis of rotation gives $I\ddot{\theta} = T_2 r - T_1 r$, where I is the moment of inertia of the pulley about the centre.

If the pulley is assumed to be a uniform disc, then
$$I = \frac{1}{2}(4m)r^2$$

Hence $T_1 - T_2 = -2mr\ddot{\theta}$ ①

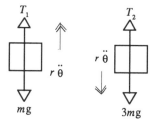

Consider the forces acting on the masses A and B. If the string does not slip, then the acceleration of A (or B) is the same as the tangential acceleration of a point on the rim of the pulley, $r\ddot{\theta}$.

The equations of motion for A and B are thus:

$$T_1 - mg = mr\ddot{\theta}$$

$$3mg - T_2 = 3mr\ddot{\theta}$$

From these equations, $T_1 - T_2 = 4mr\ddot{\theta} - 2m\,g$ ②

Equating the values of $T_1 - T_2$ from equations ① and ②,

$$-2mr\ddot{\theta} = 4mr\ddot{\theta} - 2mg \implies 6mr\ddot{\theta} = 2mg$$

$$r\ddot{\theta} = \frac{1}{3}g \approx 3.3 \text{ ms}^{-2}$$

Exercise 3

1. The moment of inertia of a flywheel is 45 kg m². It is rotating at 4 rad s⁻¹.
   Calculate its kinetic energy and its angular momentum.

2. A string is wound round a pulley of radius 0.3 metre which is free to rotate about
   a smooth vertical axis. The string is pulled horizontally with a constant force of
   48 newtons. If the moment of inertia of the pulley about the axis is 18 kg m²,
   calculate its angular acceleration. If the initial angular speed is 2 rad s⁻¹, calculate
   its angular speed after 5 seconds.

3. A uniform circular flywheel whose moment of inertia about its axis of rotation is
   60 kg m² rotates under the action of a constant torque C newton metres. If the
   flywheel starts from rest, find an equation relating the angular speed $\dot\theta$ rad s⁻¹
   with C and the time t seconds. Find also an equation relating the angular speed,
   the torque and the angle θ radians through which the flywheel has turned. If, after
   turning through 200 revolutions, its angular speed is 20 r.p.s., calculate C.

4. The flywheel of an engine is running at 100 r.p.m. The engine is then switched off
   and the flywheel takes 25 seconds to come to rest. If the moment of inertia of the
   flywheel about the axis of rotation is 500 kg m², calculate the magnitude of the
   constant retarding couple acting on the flywheel.

5. A particle P of mass m kg is hanging at the end of a light rough string. The other
   end is wrapped several times round a cylinder of radius a metres, which can rotate
   freely about its axis of symmetry.

   The moment of inertia of the cylinder
   about the axis of rotation is $3ma^2$ kg m².
   Assuming that the string does not slip on
   the cylinder, find the acceleration of P
   when the system is released from rest.

6.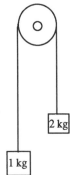
   Two masses of 1 kg and 2 kg are connected by a
   light inextensible string that passes over a
   friction-free pulley of radius 10 cm and moment
   of inertia 0.1 kg m² about its axis of rotation. The
   system is released from rest. Find the angular
   acceleration of the pulley if the string does not slip.

   2 kg

   1 kg

After working through this chapter you should:

1. know that the angular momentum (moment of momentum) of a body rotating about an axis with angular speed ω rad s^{-1} and moment of inertia I kg m^2 is $I\omega$ kg m^2 s^{-1} ;

2. know that if no external moment is applied to a system then the angular momentum of the system is conserved;

3. know that the acceleration of a point moving in a circle is:

   $r\ddot{\theta}$ tangentially in the direction of increasing θ,

   $r\dot{\theta}^2$ radially inwards towards the centre of the circle;

4. know that for a body rotating about a fixed axis, the equation of rotational motion is:

   $$\sum Fr = I\ddot{\theta}$$

   where I is the moment of inertia of the body about the axis of rotation and $\sum Fr$ is the sum of the moments of the external forces about the axis in the direction of increasing θ;

5. know that the moment of a force about an axis is sometimes known as a torque.

The windscreen wiper

Observe the motion of an actual windscreen wiper and measure the arc and the time for one complete oscillation of a blade.

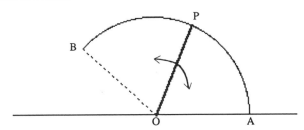

1. (a) Set up a model assuming the angular speed of P is constant.

   Use the formula

   $$\text{speed} = \frac{\text{distance APB}}{\text{time of sweep}}$$

   to estimate the speed of P.

   (b) Hence estimate the acceleration of P.

2. What is the actual speed of P at the points at the end of each sweep?

3. Set up a model using the relation $\theta = a + b \cos pt$ where a, b and p are constants.

   (a) Find suitable values for a, b and p.

   (b) Use this model to calculate the speed and acceleration of P.

4.. Compare the two models.

Flywheels

With the coming of the industrial revolution, factories and mines came to rely on power from water and steam to drive the engines and keep the wheels turning. It was found that the insertion of a massive wheel somewhere in the system could even out the fluctuations that occurred when using a variable source of power such as wind or water. These wheels, called flywheels, act as energy reservoirs, storing energy in the form of rotational energy and releasing it when the turning force is reduced. The greater the moment of inertia of the wheel, the smaller the effect of a variation in torque. This can be seen clearly in the large water-wheels of the nineteenth century. They could take as long as 15 minutes to reach full speed but, because of the flywheel effect, once this had been achieved small variations in the power supply had very little effect on the speed of the wheel.

Flywheels are part of our everyday life but, by their very nature, they are often not recognised for what they are.

An exercise bicycle may have a heavy wheel rather than a light wheel with a large retarding friction force.

A sewing machine needs a flywheel to keep the needle travelling smoothly.

(continued)

A friction-drive toy stores
energy in a flywheel to drive
it across the floor.

Record-player
turntables
are heavy.

Problem

Investigate the relationship between the moment of inertia of a flywheel about its axis of
rotation and the rate of change in angular velocity due to a given torque.

1.   Set up a simple model and use it to find this relationship. (Draw a diagram and list
       necessary variables and any simplifying assumptions you may have made.)

2.   Interpret your results.

1. The moment of inertia of a flywheel about its axis of rotation is 40 kg m². Its angular momentum is 56 kg m² s⁻¹. What is its angular speed?

2. A potter's wheel of moment of inertia 1 kg m² about its axis of rotation is spinning freely at 15 rad s⁻¹. A cylinder of clay of mass 2 kg and radius 10 cm is dropped onto the middle of the wheel. Find the new angular speed of the wheel.

3. A constant torque is applied to a bicycle wheel which is spinning freely about its axle at 6 rad s⁻¹. Its moment of inertia about the axle is 0.5 kg m². The wheel is brought to rest after 2 seconds.

    (a) Find the torque.

    (b) Through what angle has the wheel rotated?

4. A pulley has radius 15 cm and moment of inertia 0.01 kg m² about its axis of rotation. A mass of 1 kg is attached to a light string wrapped round the pulley. Initially the pulley is at rest.

    (a) Find the acceleration of the mass as it falls.

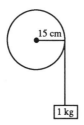

15 cm

1 kg

    (b) What is the angular speed of the pulley after half a second?

    (c) Through what distance has the mass fallen after half a second?

5 *Modelling with rigid bodies*

5.1 The force at the pivot

In this chapter you will use the equation of motion of the centre of mass of a rigid body as it moves under the action of a set of forces about a fixed axis. This will enable you to calculate the force at that axis. The photograph shows a fairground attraction – the 'pirate ship'.

> **Problem**   Find the force acting on the pivot at the top of the pirate ship.

Set up a model

Model the pirate ship and its contents as a rigid body of mass M pivoted at O with centre of mass G.

> **What external forces act on the pirate ship?**

In Chapter 4, the drawbridge was modelled as a collection of discrete particles in order to obtain the rotational equation of motion. The pirate ship will be treated in the same way.

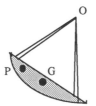

The forces acting on any particle P of mass *m* are external forces (its weight) and internal forces from adjacent particles. Suppose the resultant of these is the force **F**.

The acceleration of P will be written quite generally as $\ddot{\mathbf{r}}$. Although the path of P is known to be circular, the result to be obtained will apply to the general motion of a rigid body.

Using Newton's second law for P, $m\ddot{\mathbf{r}} = \mathbf{F}$ ①

Summing for all the particles, $\Sigma\,(m\ddot{\mathbf{r}}) = \Sigma\mathbf{F}$, where $\Sigma\mathbf{F}$ is the sum of all the external forces. (By Newton's third law, the internal forces occur in equal and opposite pairs so their sum will be zero.)

For a single particle, $m\ddot{\mathbf{r}} = \dfrac{d^2}{dt^2}(m\mathbf{r})$

(a) For the two particles m_1 and m_2 show that:

$$\Sigma\frac{d^2}{dt^2}(m\mathbf{r}) = \frac{d^2}{dt^2}\left(\Sigma\, m\mathbf{r}\right)$$

(b) What is the formula for the position vector $\mathbf{r}_G$ of the centre of mass?

Equation ① may now be written

$$\Sigma\mathbf{F} = \Sigma\,(m\ddot{\mathbf{r}}) = \Sigma\frac{d^2}{dt^2}(m\mathbf{r})$$

$$= \frac{d^2}{dt^2}\left(\Sigma\,(m\mathbf{r})\right)$$

$$= \frac{d^2}{dt^2}(M\mathbf{r}_G)$$

So

$$\Sigma\mathbf{F} = M\frac{d^2\mathbf{r}_G}{dt^2} = M\ddot{\mathbf{r}}_G$$

Newton's second law can therefore be applied to the mass centre as if all the mass of the pirate ship were at G and all the external forces acted at G.

For any rigid body, Newton's second law applies to the mass centre.

Hence $\Sigma F = M\ddot{\mathbf{r}}_G$ where ΣF is the sum of the external forces applied to the body and $\ddot{\mathbf{r}}_G$ is the acceleration of the mass centre.

To apply this result to the pirate ship, let OG = a.
G moves in a circle and so its acceleration has
components $a\dot{\theta}^2$ towards O and $a\ddot{\theta}$ tangentially in
the direction of increasing θ.

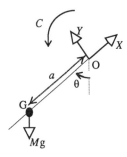

You will note that, for convenience, the force at O
is also in components in the same directions. C is
the torque due to friction (frictional couple) at the
pivot.

Using Newton's second law applied to the mass centre G,

$$X - Mg \cos \theta = Ma\dot{\theta}^2 \quad \text{towards O}$$

and $\quad Y - Mg \sin \theta = Ma\ddot{\theta} \quad$ perpendicular to OG and in the direction of increasing θ

From these equations, the external forces X and Y may be calculated.

(a) **Write down the equation of rotational motion for the
pirate ship.**

(b) **Write $I = \lambda M$ (where λ is a constant) and assume that
the frictional couple is negligible. Then show that the
component Y of the force at O is given by:**

$$Y = Mg \left(1 - \frac{a^2}{\lambda}\right) \sin \theta$$

In order to find the component X of the force at O, the angular speed $\dot{\theta}$ is required. If
there is no loss of mechanical energy, then θ may be obtained in one of two ways:

(i) from the conservation of energy equation,

or

(ii) by integrating the equation of rotational motion $I\ddot{\theta} = \Sigma (Fr)$.

Energy can only be conserved if there is no frictional couple at the pivot. (In addition,
energy losses due to air resistance, etc. must also be negligible.) If energy is lost then
$\dot{\theta}$ may only be found by integrating the equation of rotational motion, and then only if
the frictional couple is constant or given in a form that can be integrated.

You will have noted that it is most convenient to use the radial and tangential
component form of Newton's second law. This is always true if the rigid body is
rotating about a fixed axis.

In general, for a rigid body with mass centre G rotating about a fixed pivot O where OG = a,

$$\ddot{r} = \begin{bmatrix} a\dot\theta^2 \\ a\ddot\theta \end{bmatrix} \quad \text{and} \quad F = \begin{bmatrix} \Sigma F_r \\ \Sigma F_\theta \end{bmatrix}$$

the directions being indicated in the diagrams.

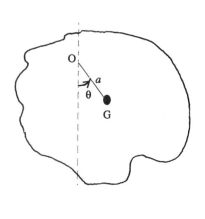

Then $F = M\ddot{r}$ for the mass centre gives $\Sigma F_r = Ma\dot\theta^2$ and $\Sigma F_\theta = Ma\ddot\theta$.

> **For a rigid body of mass M kg and mass centre G rotating about a fixed point O, where OG = a:**
>
> $\Sigma F_r = Ma\dot\theta^2$ **radially inwards,**
> $\Sigma F_\theta = Ma\ddot\theta$ **in the direction of increasing θ,**
>
> **where ΣF_r and ΣF_θ are the sums of the components in the radial and tangential directions of all the external forces acting on the body.**

Example 1

A body of mass 7 kg is rotating round a pivot. The angular speed, $\dot\theta$, is 2π rad s^{-1} when $\theta = \frac{\pi}{6}$ radians and the distance between the centre of mass and the pivot is 2 metres. Find the force on the pivot along the line joining the centre of mass to the pivot point.

Solution

Let X be the required force acting along GO.
Applying Newton's second law to the centre of mass parallel to GO,

$$X - Mg\cos\theta = Ma\dot\theta^2$$

$$X = 7 \times 2 \times (2\pi)^2 + \frac{70\sqrt3}{2}$$

$$= 613.3$$

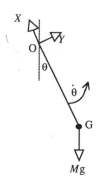

The force at the pivot along the line joining the centre of mass to the pivot point is 613 newtons (to 3 s.f.).

The next example illustrates the way that $\dot{\theta}$ can be found from the conservation of energy equation, providing there is no loss of mechanical energy.

Example 2

The pirate ship has mass 3.2 tonnes and moment of inertia 500 000 kg m² about the pivot O. Its centre of gravity is 10 metres from the pivot and the angular speed of the ship is zero when OG makes an angle of 60° to the vertical.

(a)   Calculate its angular speed when the ship is at its lowest position.

(b)   Hence find the contact force at the pivot at that time.

(c)   Find the contact force at the pivot when OG makes an angle θ with the vertical.

Solution

| Set up a model |

Assume that there is no frictional torque at the pivot point and that energy is conserved.

| Analyse |

(a)   Initial PE = 3200 x 10 x 10 (1 – cos 60°) joules
      Initial KE = 0
      Final PE = 0
      Final KE = 0.5 x 500 000$\dot{\theta}^2$

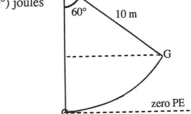

Using the energy equation,

160 000 = 250 000 $\dot{\theta}^2$ so $\dot{\theta}$ = 0.8.

When the ship is at its lowest point the angular speed is 0.8 rad s⁻¹.

(b)   Applying Newton's second law to the centre of mass gives

$$X - mg \cos \theta = ma\dot{\theta}^2 \text{ and } Y - mg \sin \theta = ma\ddot{\theta}$$

When θ = 0, X = 32 000 + 3200 x 10 x 0.64
                    = 52 480

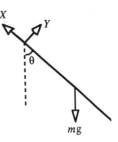

The equation of rotational motion gives

$$I\ddot{\theta} = - mgr \sin \theta$$
$$= 0$$

So $\ddot{\theta}$ = 0 and hence $Y = ma\ddot{\theta} + mg \sin \theta = 0$

The resultant force at O is 52 480 newtons along GO.

(c)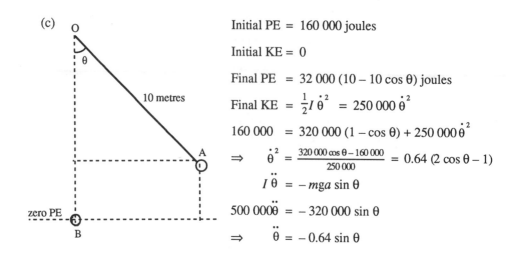

Initial PE = 160 000 joules

Initial KE = 0

Final PE = 32 000 (10 – 10 cos θ) joules

Final KE = $\frac{1}{2}I\dot{\theta}^2$ = 250 000 $\dot{\theta}^2$

160 000 = 320 000 (1 – cos θ) + 250 000$\dot{\theta}^2$

$\Rightarrow \quad \dot{\theta}^2 = \frac{320\,000\cos\theta - 160\,000}{250\,000}$ = 0.64 (2 cos θ – 1)

$I\ddot{\theta} = -mga \sin \theta$

500 000$\ddot{\theta}$ = – 320 000 sin θ

$\Rightarrow \quad \ddot{\theta}$ = – 0.64 sin θ

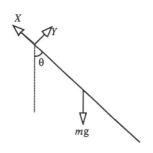

$Y - mg \sin \theta = ma\ddot{\theta}$

$Y = -32\,000 \times 0.64 \sin \theta + 32\,000 \sin \theta$

$= 11\,520 \sin \theta$

$X - mg \cos \theta = ma\dot{\theta}^2$

$X = 32\,000 \cos \theta + 20\,480 (2 \cos \theta - 1)$

$= 72\,960 \cos \theta - 20\,480$

$$\begin{bmatrix} X \\ Y \end{bmatrix} = \begin{bmatrix} 72\,960 \cos \theta - 20\,480 \\ 11\,520 \sin \theta \end{bmatrix}$$

Interpret

By plotting the graph of $\sqrt{(X^2 + Y^2)}$ against θ on a graphic calculator you can see that the magnitude of the force varies from 52 480 newtons when the ship is at its lowest point to 18 860 newtons when the ship is at its highest point, with OG at an angle of 60° to the vertical. The force decreases as the ship gets higher.

$Y = 0$ at B indicates that the centre of mass has no tangential acceleration at B and this is indeed the case.

Exercise 1

1. A bauble is modelled as a hollow sphere of radius
    5 cm and mass 0.05 kg, with a tiny loop of light
    wire on its surface. The bauble is hanging by the
    loop from a smooth branch and swings to and fro
    with a line from the loop through the centre of the
    sphere making a maximum angle of 20° to the
    vertical.

    Calculate the magnitude of the reaction force acting on the branch when the
    bauble is in this extreme position.

2.

A large door 1.2 metres wide and 2 metres high is hinged 0.2 metre from one edge.
The door has mass 40 kg and when it is opened a spring mechanism applies a constant
restoring couple to close it.

In an experiment, the times for the door to close when opened at different angles were
recorded.

Angle ($\theta°$)	10	20	40	60	80
Time (seconds)	1.1	1.5	2.1	2.6	3.0

(a) Find an expression for θ (radians) in terms of t.

(b) Hence find an expression for $\ddot{\theta}$.

(c) Calculate the moment of inertia of the door about the hinge. Hence find the
     magnitude of the restoring couple.

(d) Assuming there are no frictional forces, calculate the angular speed of the door
     when it has closed through 80°.

75

3. A huge standing stone has gradually tilted so it is at 30° to the vertical. A fly lands on the block and the stone starts to topple. The stone is not uniform but can be modelled as a rod of length 4 metres and mass 1.5 tonnes, with centre of mass at the mid point and moment of inertia about the base of 8000 kg m².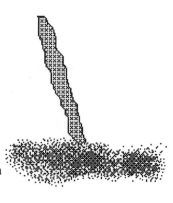

   Assuming that the stone rotates freely about its base, calculate the magnitude and direction of the reaction force when it makes an angle of 45° to the vertical.

4. A simple pendulum consists of a light rod of length 70 cm with a bob of mass 2 kg attached to one end. The other end is tied to a smooth hook. The motion of the pendulum is described by the equation $\theta = 0.2 \sin 2\pi t$. where θ radians is the angle between the pendulum and the downwards vertical at time t.

   Find expressions for the radial and tangential components of the reaction force at the hook in terms of θ. Calculate these components when θ is 0.1745 (i.e. when the pendulum is at 10° to the vertical).

5E. A ruler 30 cm long and of mass 0.06 kg is balanced on one end, on a rough horizontal table. It is slightly displaced from the vertical so that it topples over. Assume that friction is sufficient to prevent slipping and assume that the ruler can be modelled as a uniform rod.

   (a) Find expressions for   (i) $\ddot{\theta}$ (ii) $\dot{\theta}$

   when the ruler is at angle θ to the vertical.

   You may find it helpful to use the result

   $$\ddot{\theta} = \frac{d\dot{\theta}}{dt} = \frac{d\dot{\theta}}{d\theta} \times \frac{d\theta}{dt} = \dot{\theta} \times \frac{d\dot{\theta}}{d\theta}$$

   (b) When $\theta = 15°$, calculate the magnitude and direction of the reaction force acting at the base.

   (c) Find the least value of the coefficient of friction to prevent slipping when $\theta = 15°$.

76

5.2 Modelling rigid body motion

Working through the text you will have seen many rigid bodies whose motion you could model. It is important to be clear **when** the various possible models are applicable.

You can model a body as a particle when its overall size is small compared with the path of its motion. The moon going round the earth can, for most purposes, be modelled as a particle. A tree falling could be modelled as a particle but the solution given would be inaccurate and a much better solution would be obtained by treating it as a rigid body rotating around a fixed point. It is important that you realise that all the work so far has been in modelling rigid bodies rotating around a fixed axis. The motion of a body that rotates as it travels along, like a wheel rolling along the ground, is outside the scope of the unit. It is interesting to note that the ideas on rotation covered in this unit hold for a body rotating about its centre of mass, even if the centre of mass is moving. You should not, however, try to use such a complex situation for your project.

> **Which of the situations below can you model as:**
>
> (a)   **particle motion;**
>
> (b)   **rigid body motion about a fixed axis;**
>
> (c)   **a rigid body in equilibrium?**

77

A great many interesting situations can be modelled using the mathematics you have learnt. The following may give you some ideas for projects.

Some large supermarkets have revolving doors. Investigate their design, bearing in mind that they must allow a shopper with a trolley to pass and that queuing should be minimised.

Factory chimneys can be demolished by removing the bricks at the base on one side so that they topple. They often appear to break when halfway down. Why?

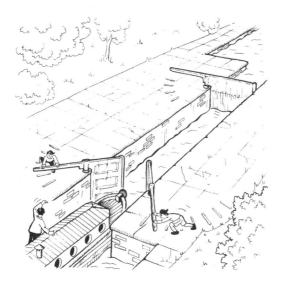

Locks are used to enable boats to move from one water level to another. You could investigate how the forces on a lock-gate change as the water level drops. Why do you think there are two gates at one end and one at the other?

Cricket rollers are often designed to have the handle above the roller. Why?

For centuries, animals have been used to lift water. Investigate how this is done.

After working through this chapter you should:

1. know that for a rigid body, Newton's second law applies to its mass centre, that is $\mathbf{F} = m\,\ddot{\mathbf{r}}$ where $\mathbf{F}$ is the sum of all the forces applied to the body and $\ddot{\mathbf{r}}$ is the acceleration of the mass centre;

2. know that for a rigid body rotating about a fixed pivot, the best directions in which to resolve are radially and tangentially. Thus for a rigid body of mass M kg and mass centre G rotating about a fixed point O, where $OG = a$

    $$\Sigma F_r = Ma\dot{\theta}^2 \text{ radially inwards,}$$

    $$\Sigma F_\theta = Ma\ddot{\theta} \text{ in the direction of increasing } \theta,$$

    where ΣF_r and ΣF_θ are the sums of the components of all the external forces acting on the body;

3. know that if there is no external torque acting then the rotational energy is conserved.

Tutorial sheet

1. A gymnast balances on her hands on a high bar. She starts to swing down, keeping her body and arms straight.

    Find the magnitude of the force on her hands both when she is horizontal and when she is at the lowest point of the swing, if she is modelled:

    (a) as a particle of mass 60 kg on a light rod a distance 1 metre from the point of rotation;

    (b) as a uniform rod of length 2 metres and mass 60 kg rotating about one end.

2. The tail-gate of a delivery lorry can be modelled as a uniform rectangular lamina 3 metres by 1.5 metres, of mass 200 kg, which rotates about an axis along one edge as shown.

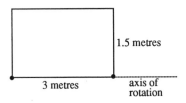

1.5 metres

3 metres

axis of
rotation

    The tail-gate is displaced from the vertical and starts to swing down, rotating freely about the hinges.

    (a) Find the radial and tangential components of the reaction force at the hinges when the gate makes an angle of θ with the upward vertical.

    (b) Find the angular speed of the tail-gate when it is at its lowest point.

    (c) What is the contact force at the hinges in this position?

SOLUTIONS

1 Forces and couples

1.1 Introduction

> **What extra condition is needed for a rigid body to be in equilibrium?**

The forces must not have a turning effect on the body. Thus the sum of their moments about an axis must be zero.

> **In reality, the wall is unlikely to be completely smooth. How does this affect the validity of the model?**

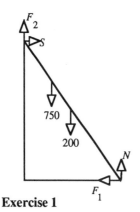

The ladder will try to slip down the wall, so the friction on the ladder from the wall will act upwards. Common sense would tell you that this makes it possible for the man to climb higher. Does this really happen?

After completing this chapter, you will be able to combine forces and hence reduce the number of forces you need to consider. You might find this a good starting point for an investigation.

Exercise 1

1.

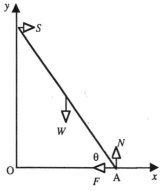

Taking axes with origin at O, since the ladder is in equilibrium,

$$\begin{bmatrix} S \\ 0 \end{bmatrix} + \begin{bmatrix} -F \\ 0 \end{bmatrix} + \begin{bmatrix} 0 \\ N \end{bmatrix} + \begin{bmatrix} 0 \\ -W \end{bmatrix} = 0$$

$$\Rightarrow S = F, \ W = N$$

Taking moments about A, the foot of the ladder,

$$S \times 4 \sin \theta - W \times 2 \cos \theta = 0$$

$$\Rightarrow S = \frac{1}{2}W \cot \theta$$

$$\Rightarrow F = \frac{1}{2}W \cot \theta$$

For equilibrium, $F \leq \mu N$

i.e. $\frac{1}{2} W \cot \theta \leq \frac{1}{2} W$

$\Rightarrow \qquad \cot \theta \leq 1$

$\Rightarrow \qquad \theta \geq 45°$

The ladder must be inclined at an angle of at least 45° to the horizontal.

2.

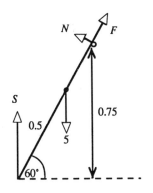

The stick is modelled as a uniform rod.
Taking moments clockwise about the rail,

$$S \times \frac{0.75}{\tan 60°} - 5 \times \left(\frac{0.75}{\tan 60°} - 0.5 \cos 60° \right) = 0$$

$$S \times 0.433 - 5 \times 0.183 = 0$$
$$S = 2.11 \text{ newtons}$$

Taking axes along and perpendicular to the walking stick,

$$\begin{bmatrix} S \cos 30° \\ S \sin 30° \end{bmatrix} + \begin{bmatrix} F \\ 0 \end{bmatrix} + \begin{bmatrix} -5 \cos 30° \\ -5 \sin 30° \end{bmatrix} + \begin{bmatrix} 0 \\ N \end{bmatrix} = 0$$

$$\Rightarrow F = 5 \cos 30° - S \cos 30° = 2.5 \text{ newtons}$$
$$N = 5 \sin 30° - S \sin 30° = 1.445 \text{ newtons}$$
$$F \leq \mu N$$
$$\Rightarrow \mu \geq \frac{F}{N} = \frac{2.5}{1.445} = 1.73$$

3. Assume that the legs of the table are positioned as shown.
By Pythagoras' theorem, $a^2 + a^2 = r^2$

$$\Rightarrow b = r - a = r - \frac{r\sqrt{2}}{2} = r\left(\frac{2 - \sqrt{2}}{2} \right)$$

Taking moments about X,
$$50a = Fb$$
$$\Rightarrow 50\frac{\sqrt{2}}{2} = F\left(\frac{2 - \sqrt{2}}{2} \right)$$
$$\Rightarrow F \approx 120.7$$

The minimum force is 120.7 newtons,
so the least mass is 12.1 kilograms.

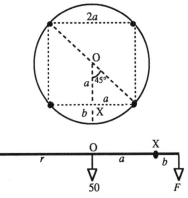

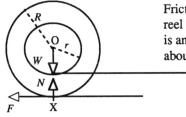

4.

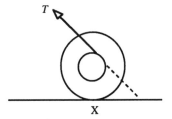

Friction acts through X, the point of contact of the
reel with the lawn. Taking moments about X, there
is an unbalanced moment of $T(R - r)$ clockwise
about X. The reel will therefore roll to the right.

If the reel is to roll the other way then the
hose must exert an anticlockwise moment
moment about X. Hence it must be pulled so
that the line of action of the pull passes to the
right of the point of contact with the lawn.

5. Taking moments about A,

$S \times 2 \times \sin 60° - 200 \times 1 \times \cos 60° - 1000 \times 2 \times \cos 60° = 0$

$\Rightarrow S\sqrt{3} = 1100$

$S = \frac{1}{3}1100\sqrt{3} = 635.1$ newtons

$$\begin{bmatrix} S \\ 0 \end{bmatrix} + \begin{bmatrix} -F \\ 0 \end{bmatrix} + \begin{bmatrix} 0 \\ R \end{bmatrix} + \begin{bmatrix} 0 \\ -200 \end{bmatrix} + \begin{bmatrix} 0 \\ -1000 \end{bmatrix} = 0$$

$\Rightarrow R = 1200$ and $F = S = 635.1$

$F \le \mu R \Rightarrow 635.1 \le 1200\mu$

$\Rightarrow \mu \ge 0.53$

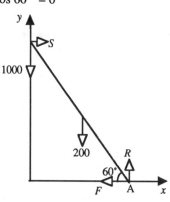

6.

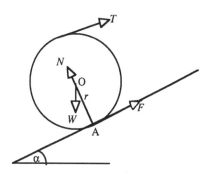

$F \le \mu N$, so $\frac{1}{2}W \sin \alpha \le \mu W \cos \alpha$

$\Rightarrow \mu \ge \frac{1}{2}\tan \alpha$

Taking moments about A,

$2rT = Wr \sin \alpha$

$T = \frac{1}{2}W \sin \alpha$

Taking moments about O,

$Tr = Fr$

$\Rightarrow T = F = \frac{1}{2}W \sin \alpha$

Resolving forces perpendicular to the plane,

$N = W \cos \alpha$

7. As the plank is about to leave the ground, the reaction is at A.
Taking moments about A,

$W \times l = T \times 2l \cos \alpha$

$\Rightarrow T = \frac{1}{2}\dfrac{W}{\cos \alpha}$

Resolving horizontally,

$F = T \sin \alpha = \frac{1}{2}W \tan \alpha$

Resolving vertically,

$N + T \cos \alpha = W$

Hence $N = W - \frac{1}{2}\dfrac{W}{\cos \alpha} \cos \alpha = \frac{1}{2}W$

$F \le \mu N$

$\Rightarrow \frac{1}{2}W \tan \alpha \le \mu \frac{1}{2}W$

$\Rightarrow \mu \ge \tan \alpha$

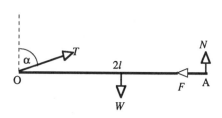

1.2 Normal contact forces and rigid bodies

> The line of action of the contact force **R**, where **R** = **N** + **F**,
> passes through the mid-point of AB. Why is this?

If **N** and **F** are replaced by **R**, the force diagram shows there are only 3 forces acting:
P = 30 newtons horizontally, **W** = 300 newtons vertically and **R**. The case is in equilibrium so the forces are either parallel or meet at a point. **P** and **W** meet at the mid-point of AB, so **R** must also pass through that point.

Exercise 2

1. The case is in equilibrium so $\begin{bmatrix} 100 - F \\ N - 400 \end{bmatrix} = 0$.

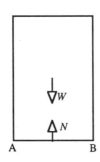

$$\Rightarrow N = 400, \quad F = 100$$

Taking moments about C,

$$100 \times 1.5 + Nx - 400 \times \frac{0.75}{2} = 0$$

$$\Rightarrow 100 \times 1.5 + 400x - 200 \times 0.75 = 0$$
$$400x = 0$$
$$x = 0$$

The reaction is acting at C. A slightly harder push would cause the case to topple about C.

2.

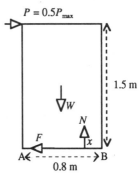

(a) The normal contact force acts through the mid-point of AB.

(b) The normal contact force acts at B.
Taking moments about B, $P_{max} \times 1.5 - W \times 0.4 = 0$

$$\Rightarrow \qquad P_{max} = \frac{4}{15}W$$

(c) The normal contact force acts at a distance x metres from B.
Taking moments about B,

$$\frac{1}{2}P_{max} \times 1.5 + Nx - W \times 0.4 = 0 \quad \text{where } \frac{1}{2}P_{max} = \frac{2}{15}W$$
$$0.2W + Nx - 0.4W = 0$$

But $N = W$, so $x = 0.2$.

If $P > P_{max}$, the packing case slips or rotates about the edge through B.

1.3   Couples

Exercise 3

1. Let PQRS be drawn clockwise as shown.
    Clockwise moment of couple
            formed by 3N forces = 6 Nm
    Clockwise moment of couple
            formed by 5N forces = 10 Nm
    Resultant couple = 10 + 6 = 16 Nm clockwise

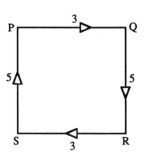

2. The least force, F, is needed when the push is as shown.
    Taking moments about the hinge,
    $$15 - 0.75 \times F = 0$$
    $$\Rightarrow \qquad F = \frac{15}{0.75} = 20$$
    The least force is 20 newtons.

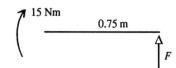

3.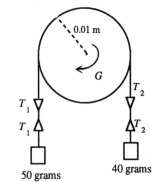

    50 grams   40 grams

    The system is in a state of equilibrium, so
    $$T_1 = 0.05g = 0.5 \text{ newton}$$
    $$T_2 = 0.04g = 0.4 \text{ newton}$$
    Taking moments about O,
    $$G = T_1 \times 0.01 - T_2 \times 0.01$$
    $$= 0.001 \text{ Nm}$$

4. Using the method of question 3,
    $$3 = (T_1 - T_2) \times 0.15$$
    $$T_1 - T_2 = 20$$
    The difference in tensions must be greater than 20 newtons.

1.4   Resultant forces and couples

(a)   Find the resultant force acting on the particle.

(b)   The same forces are acting on this lamina, which has the same
       mass as the particle.

       Why might the effect be different from that in (a)?

(a)

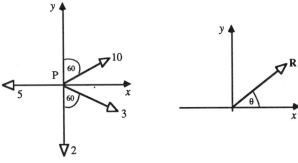

Taking axes with origin at P, as shown,

$$R = \begin{bmatrix} -5 \\ 0 \end{bmatrix} + \begin{bmatrix} 10 \sin 60° \\ 10 \cos 60° \end{bmatrix} + \begin{bmatrix} 3 \sin 60° \\ -3 \cos 60° \end{bmatrix} + \begin{bmatrix} 0 \\ -2 \end{bmatrix} = \begin{bmatrix} 6.26 \\ 1.5 \end{bmatrix} \quad \text{acting at P}$$

$R = 6.44$ newtons (to 2 d.p.), $\theta = 13.5°$

(b) In case (a), the particle will accelerate along the line of action of the resultant force. In case (b), although the magnitude and direction of the resultant force can be calculated, you do not know where it will act. The lamina may therefore move off in a straight line and/or rotate.

Exercise 4

1.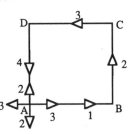

$$R = \begin{bmatrix} 1 \\ 0 \end{bmatrix} + \begin{bmatrix} 0 \\ 2 \end{bmatrix} + \begin{bmatrix} -3 \\ 0 \end{bmatrix} + \begin{bmatrix} 0 \\ -4 \end{bmatrix} = \begin{bmatrix} -2 \\ -2 \end{bmatrix}$$

The force is of 2.83 N, at 45° to BA, downwards.
If a is the side of the square,
$G = 3a + 2a = 5a$
The couple is $5a$ Nm anticlockwise.

2.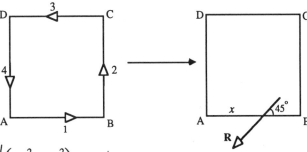

$R = \sqrt{\left((-2)^2 + (-2)^2\right)} = 2\sqrt{2}$ at 45° to BA.
Taking moments about A,
$2a + 3a = -2\sqrt{2} \times x \sin 45°$
$5a = -2x \Rightarrow -x = \frac{5}{2}a$

i.e. the resultant force would act at a point $\frac{5}{2}a$
from A, on BA produced.

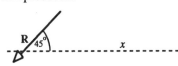

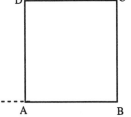

3. Using conventional axes,

$$\mathbf{R} = \begin{bmatrix} 1 \\ 0 \end{bmatrix} + \begin{bmatrix} 0 \\ -2 \end{bmatrix} + \begin{bmatrix} -3 \\ 0 \end{bmatrix} + \begin{bmatrix} 0 \\ 4 \end{bmatrix} + \begin{bmatrix} 2 \\ -2 \end{bmatrix}$$

$$= 0$$

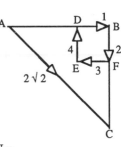

The resultant force is zero. Therefore the system reduces to a couple or is in static equilibrium.

Taking moments about B,

$G = 2\sqrt{2} \times 3 \times \sin 45° - 3 \times 1 - 4 \times 1 = -1$

The system is equivalent to a clockwise couple of 1 Nm.

4.

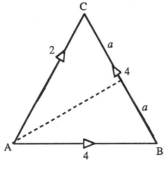

$$\mathbf{R} = \begin{bmatrix} 4 \\ 0 \end{bmatrix} + \begin{bmatrix} -4 \cos 60° \\ 4 \sin 60° \end{bmatrix} + \begin{bmatrix} 2 \cos 60° \\ 2 \sin 60° \end{bmatrix} = \begin{bmatrix} 3 \\ 3\sqrt{3} \end{bmatrix}$$

$$\Rightarrow R = \sqrt{\left(3^2 + (3\sqrt{3})^2\right)} = 6$$

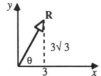

$\tan \theta = \dfrac{3\sqrt{3}}{3} = \sqrt{3}$

$\theta = 60°$

So the line of action of **R** is parallel to AC.

Taking moments about A,

$4 \times a\sqrt{3} = Rx \sin 60°$

$4 \times a\sqrt{3} = 6x \dfrac{\sqrt{3}}{2}$

$\Rightarrow \quad x = \dfrac{4}{3}a$

i.e. the line of action of **R** passes through the point of trisection of AB nearer to B.

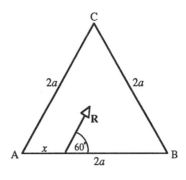

5.

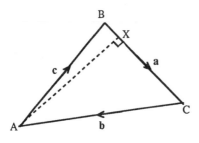

$\mathbf{R} = \mathbf{a} + \mathbf{b} + \mathbf{c}$

$= \overrightarrow{BC} + \overrightarrow{CA} + \overrightarrow{AB}$

$= 0$

Hence the system reduces to a couple.

Taking moments about A,

$G = a \times AX$, but $AX = AB \sin B$, so

$G = ac \sin B$

$= 2 \times \dfrac{1}{2} ac \sin B$

$= 2 \times$ area of triangle ABC

2 *Toppling or sliding?*

2.1 Introduction

Exercise 1

1. (a) The cube is in equilibrium under
   three forces, as shown.

   It will not slide if $F < \mu N$.
   The resultant force is zero, so

   $$F = W \sin \alpha, \quad N = W \cos \alpha$$

   Hence $\tan \alpha < \mu$

   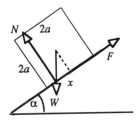

   The cube will not topple if

   $$\tan \alpha = \frac{x}{a} < \frac{a}{a} = 1$$

   The cube will topple before it slides if $\mu > 1$.

   (b)

   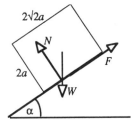

   Using the same method, the cube will
   topple before it slides if $\mu > \sqrt{2}$.

2.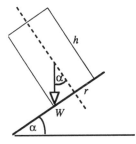

On the point of toppling,

$$\tan \alpha = \frac{r}{\frac{1}{2}h} = \frac{2r}{h}$$

$$\tan \beta = 2 \tan \alpha$$

$$\Rightarrow \frac{r}{l} = \frac{4r}{h}$$

$$\Rightarrow l = \frac{1}{4}h$$

On the point of toppling,

$$\tan \beta = \frac{r}{l}$$

The centre of gravity of the cone is a quarter of the way up its height.

3. When the case is about to topple, N passes through A.
Taking moments about A gives $2aP = aW$.
Sliding occurs if $P > F$ and $F = \mu N = \mu W$.
Then:

$$W < 2\mu W$$
$$\mu < 0.5$$

Toppling occurs first if $P = F > 0.5W$ and $F < \mu W$.
$$0.5W < \mu W$$
$$\mu > 0.5$$

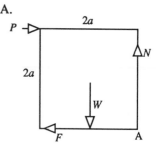

4.

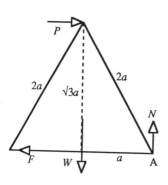

The prism is on the point of toppling when N acts at A. Let the edge of the prism be $2a$.
Taking moments about A, $Pa\sqrt{3} = Wa$

$$\Rightarrow P = \frac{\sqrt{3}}{3}W$$

The prism is on the point of sliding if $F = \mu N$.
But by Newton's second law,
$$P - F = 0 \quad \text{and} \quad W - N = 0$$

So $P = \mu W$

Hence if the prism is to slide before it tilts,

$$\mu < \frac{\sqrt{3}}{3}$$

2.2   Centres of mass and centres of gravity

Exercise 2

1. The volume of each slice $= \pi y^2 \, \delta x$
The mass of each slice $= \rho \pi y^2 \, \delta x$,

where ρ is the mass per unit volume.

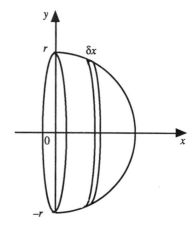

Let the centre of mass be at $(\bar{x}, 0)$.
Then taking moments about $0y$,

$$\bar{x} \sum_{x=0}^{r} \rho \pi y^2 \, \delta x = \sum_{x=0}^{r} x \rho \pi y^2 \, \delta x$$

$\rho \pi$ is constant, so in the limit,

$$\bar{x} \int_0^r y^2 \, dx = \int_0^r x y^2 \, dx$$

But $x^2 + y^2 = r^2$, so $\bar{x} \int_0^r (r^2 - x^2) \, dx = \int_0^r x(r^2 - x^2) \, dx$

$$\bar{x} \left[r^2 x - \frac{x^3}{3} \right]_0^r = \left[\frac{r^2 x^2}{2} - \frac{x^4}{4} \right]_0^r$$

$$\Rightarrow \frac{2}{3} r^3 \bar{x} = \frac{1}{4} r^4 \Rightarrow \bar{x} = \frac{3}{8} r$$

2. (a)

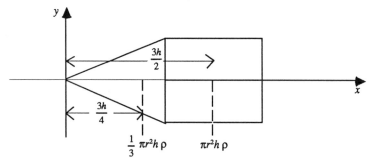

Mass of the cone $= \frac{1}{3}\pi r^2 h\rho,$ where ρ = mass per unit volume

Centre of mass of the cone is $\frac{3}{4}h$ from the vertex.

Mass of cylinder $= \pi r^2 h\rho$

The centre of mass is $\frac{1}{2}h$ from the circular end, i.e. $\frac{3}{2}h$ from vertex of cone.

Then the centre of mass is at $(\bar{x}, 0)$, where axes are as shown.

$$\left(\frac{1}{3}\pi r^2 h\rho + \pi r^2 h\rho\right)\bar{x} = \frac{1}{3}\pi r^2 h\rho \times \frac{3h}{4} + \pi r^2 h\rho \times \frac{3h}{2}$$

$$\frac{4}{3}\bar{x} = \frac{h}{4} + \frac{3h}{2}$$

$$\bar{x} = \frac{21}{16}h$$

(b)

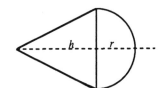

Use the same notation and method as in (a).

Taking moments about the free face of the cylinder,

$$\left(\pi r^2 h\rho + \frac{2}{3}\pi r^3 \rho\right)\bar{x} = \pi r^2 h\rho \times \frac{1}{2}h + \frac{2}{3}\pi r^3 \rho \times \left(h + \frac{3}{8}r\right)$$

$$\left(h + \frac{2}{3}r\right)\bar{x} = \frac{1}{2}h^2 + \frac{2}{3}r\left(h + \frac{3}{8}r\right)$$

$$\Rightarrow \bar{x} = \frac{6h^2 + 8rh + 3r^2}{4(3h + 2r)}$$

3.

From the worked example in the text,

$$\bar{x} = \frac{3h^2 + 8rh + 3r^2}{4(h + 2r)}$$

The centre of gravity must be in the hemisphere if the toy is to return to the upright position. So,

$$\frac{3h^2 + 8rh + 3r^2}{4(h + 2r)} > h$$

$\Rightarrow 3h^2 + 8rh + 3r^2 > 4h^2 + 8rh$

$\Rightarrow \qquad\qquad 3r^2 > h^2$

$\Rightarrow \qquad\qquad h < r\sqrt{3}$

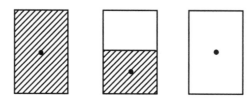

4.

As the level of cola initally drops, so the centre of mass also drops, though not as quickly. By the end of the evening, the centre of mass is back in the centre of the can and so there is a position in which the centre of mass is just in the surface of the liquid remaining.

To consider this position, you might find it easiest to imagine the cola as a solid and then tip the can on its side and balance it at its centre of mass.

If more liquid is added, the can would rotate clockwise. If some liquid is removed, then this makes it lighter on the left and so the can would again rotate clockwise. In both cases, the centre of mass moves to the right.

Hence the centre of mass is at its lowest point when it is just in the surface of the liquid. Making some assumptions about relative densities of cola and aluminium, can you confirm this argument?

3 *Rotation and energy*

3.1 Rotational energy

> **Why does this formula imply that it is easier to push on the outside edge of the door?**

If the work needed to turn the door through a given angle is constant, then as r increases, F decreases. The further from the pivot he pushes, the less the force needed. If he pushes at the pivot, then no matter how hard he pushes the door will not rotate.

Exercise 1

1. $\omega = 78$ r.p.m. $= \frac{78 \times 2\pi}{60}$ rad s^{-1},

    Rotational KE $= \frac{1}{2} I \omega^2$

    $\qquad = \frac{0.05 \times (78 \times 2\pi)^2}{60^2}$

    $\qquad = 3.34$ joules

2. Work done = change in rotational KE

    $\qquad = \frac{1}{2} \times 0.05 \times 40^2 - 0$

    $\qquad = 40$ joules

    Work done = 40 joules

3. Initial rotational KE $= \frac{1}{2} I \times 10^2$

    $\qquad\qquad = 50\,I$

    Final rotational KE $= \frac{1}{2} I \times 5^2$

    $\qquad\qquad = 12\frac{1}{2} I$

    But $50\,I - 12.5\,I = 1000$

    $\Rightarrow I = 26.7$ kg m^2

4.

The rod has no mass so its moment of inertia is zero. The rotational KE of each particle is $\frac{1}{2}m(r\,\omega)^2$.

$$\text{Total KE} = [\tfrac{1}{2} \times 0.01 \times (1 \times 4)^2] \times 2$$

$$= 0.16 \text{ joule}$$

5. **(a)**

$$\text{Total KE} = \frac{1}{2}\frac{m}{3}\left(\frac{d\omega}{2}\right)^2 + \frac{1}{2}\frac{m}{3}(d\omega)^2$$

$$= \frac{1}{2}\frac{m}{3}d^2\omega^2\left[\frac{1}{4} + 1\right]$$

$$= \frac{5md^2\omega^2}{24}$$

(b)

$$\text{Total KE} = \frac{1}{2}\frac{m}{5}\left(\frac{d\omega}{4}\right)^2 + \frac{1}{2}\frac{m}{5}\left(\frac{2d}{4}\,\omega\right)^2 + \frac{1}{2}\frac{m}{5}\left(\frac{3d}{4}\,\omega\right)^2 + \frac{1}{2}\frac{m}{5}(d\omega)^2$$

$$= \frac{md^2\omega^2}{10}\left[\left(\tfrac{1}{4}\right)^2 + \left(\tfrac{2}{4}\right)^2 + \left(\tfrac{3}{4}\right)^2 + \left(\tfrac{4}{4}\right)^2\right]$$

$$= \frac{3}{16}md^2\omega^2$$

(c)

$$\text{Total KE} = \frac{1}{2}\frac{m}{101}\left(\frac{d\omega}{100}\right)^2 + \ldots = \frac{md^2\omega^2}{2020000}(1^2 + 2^2 + \ldots + 100^2)$$

$$1^2 + 2^2 + \ldots + 100^2 = \frac{1}{6} \times 100 \times 101 \times 201$$

and so the total KE is $0.1675\,md^2\omega^2$

You will notice in the answers to (a), (b) and (c) a decreasing sequence of coefficients $\frac{5}{24}$, $\frac{3}{16}$, 0.1675.

As n increases this sequence converges; you may like to find its limiting value.

6. Assuming that the mass of cotton that unwinds can be ignored,
$\mathbf{F} = 2$, $\mathbf{r} = 0.05$ and $\theta = 2\pi$.

Work done $= 2 \times 0.05 \times 2\pi$

$\qquad = 0.628$ joule

The initial KE is zero so the KE after 1 revolution is 0.628 joule.

$$KE = \tfrac{1}{2}I\omega^2 \implies 0.628 = \tfrac{1}{2} \times 0.0003 \times \omega^2$$

$$\omega = 64.7 \text{ rad s}^{-1}$$

3.2   Moment of inertia

Exercise 2

1.   (a)

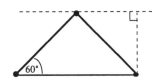

Moment of inertia $= 1 \times 0^2 + 1 \times \left(\tfrac{\sqrt{3}}{2}\right)^2 \times 2$

$\qquad = \tfrac{3}{2} \text{ kg m}^2$

(b)

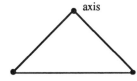

Moment of inertia $= 1 \times 0^2 + 1 \times 1^2 + 1 \times 1^2$

$\qquad = 2 \text{ kg m}^2$

(c)

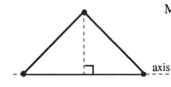

Moment of inertia $= 1 \times 0^2 + 1 \times 0^2 + 1 \times \left(\tfrac{\sqrt{3}}{2}\right)^2$

$\qquad = \tfrac{3}{4} \text{ kg m}^2$

2.

Each element of the cylinder is a distance
r from the axis.
Moment of inertia $= Mr^2$

3. (a)

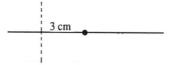

Mass per unit length is $\frac{0.010}{0.1} = 0.1$ kg per metre.

Moment of inertia $= \displaystyle\int_{-0.02}^{0.08} 0.1x^2\,dx = \left[\frac{0.1x^3}{3}\right]_{-0.02}^{0.08}$

$= 1.73 \times 10^{-5}$ kg m²

(b)

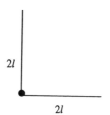

Moment of inertia of small rod about right-hand end is $\frac{4}{3} \times 0.002 \times 0.01^2$.

Moment of inertia of long rod about left-hand end is $\frac{4}{3} \times 0.008 \times 0.04^2$.

Moment of inertia of combined rod $= \frac{4}{3} \times 0.002 \times 0.01^2 + \frac{4}{3} \times 0.008 \times 0.04^2$

$= 1.73 \times 10^{-5}$ kg m²

4. Moment of inertia of a solid sphere about an axis through its centre is $\frac{2}{5}Mr^2$.

Moment of inertia $= \frac{2}{5} \times 5 \times (0.2)^2 = 0.08$ kg m²

5.

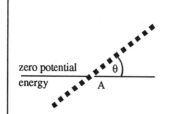

$2l$

$2l$

Moment of inertia of each rod is $\frac{4}{3}Ml^2$.

Total moment of inertia is $\frac{8}{3}Ml^2$.

3.3 Conservation of mechanical energy

zero potential energy

θ

A

(a) Find the gravitational potential energy of a rod of length 2*d* metres relative to a line through its mid-point A.

Model the rod by a set of *n* particles, each of mass $\frac{M}{n}$, equally spaced along the rod.

(b) Does its gravitational potential energy depend on the angle of slope, θ, of the rod to the horizontal?

(a) For each particle which is $x \sin \theta$ above the zero level of potential energy and has potential energy $\frac{M}{n} x \sin \theta$, there will be a matching particle below the level of zero potential energy with potential energy $-\frac{M}{n} x \sin \theta$.

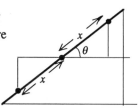

Summing, you can see that the total potential energy of the rod is

$$\sum \left(\frac{M}{n} x \sin \theta - \frac{M}{n} x \sin \theta \right) = 0$$

(b) The potential energy is zero regardless of the value of θ. Thus the orientation does not alter its potential energy.

Exercise 3

1.

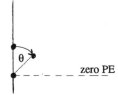

The moment of inertia of the pencil is

$$\frac{4}{3} m \times 0.075^2 = 0.0075m$$

Initial PE $= m \, g \times 0.075$
Initial KE $= 0$
Final PE $= 0$
Final KE $= \frac{1}{2} I \, \omega^2$

Since mechanical energy is conserved,

$$0.075 \, m \, g = \frac{0.0075m \, \omega^2}{2}$$
$$\Rightarrow \omega^2 = 20 \, g \approx 200$$
$$\Rightarrow \omega \approx 14.1 \text{ rad s}^{-1}$$

2.

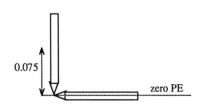

The barrier can be modelled as two rods of lengths 4 metres and 1 metre and masses 16 kg and 4 kg, pivoted at their ends. The moment of inertia of the combined barrier about the pivot is therefore:

$$\frac{4}{3} \times 16 \times 2^2 + \frac{4}{3} \times 4 \times \left(\frac{1}{2} \right)^2 = \frac{260}{3} \text{ kg m}^2$$

Initially, the centre of gravity is 1.5 m above the pivot.

Initial PE $= 20 \times 1.5g$ Final PE $= 0$
Initial KE $= 0$ Final KE $= \frac{1}{2} I \omega^2$

Assuming that no energy is lost at the pivot or against air resistance,

$$30 \, g = \frac{130}{3} \omega^2$$
$$\omega = 2.63 \text{ rad s}^{-1}$$

3.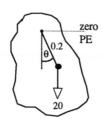

Let the moment of inertia of the body about the axis of rotation be I.

Initial PE $= -20 \times 0.2 \cos \theta$ Initial KE $= 0$

Final PE $= -20 \times 0.2$ Final KE $= \frac{1}{2} I \omega^2$

$$\frac{1}{2} I \omega^2 = 20 \times 0.2 (1 - \cos \theta)$$

$$I = \frac{8(1 - \cos \theta)}{\omega^2} \qquad \text{①}$$

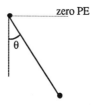

The energy equation for the particle is:

$$\frac{1}{2} \times 2 \times \omega^2 \times 0.3^2 = 20 \times 0.3 (1 - \cos \theta) \Rightarrow \omega^2 = \frac{20(1 - \cos \theta)}{0.3}$$

Substituting this value of ω^2 into ①,

$$I = \frac{8(1 - \cos \theta) \times 0.3}{20(1 - \cos \theta)} = 0.12 \text{ kg m}^2$$

4. (a)

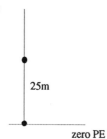

Initial PE $= 2000 \times 10 \times 25$ Final PE $= 0$

Initial KE $= 0$ Final KE $= \frac{1}{2} I \omega^2$

If the tree is modelled as a rod, $I = \frac{4}{3} \times 2000 \times 25^2$

$$= \frac{5\,000\,000}{3}$$

By conservation of mechanical energy,

$$\frac{1}{2} \times \frac{5\,000\,000}{3} \times \omega^2 = 500\,000$$

$$\omega \approx 0.775 \text{ rad s}^{-1}$$

(b) $v = \omega r \approx 38.7 \text{ ms}^{-1}$

(c) A tree may be either heavier at the bottom than at the top, for example a fir tree, or heavier at the top than at the bottom, for example an oak tree.

Taking the first case and exaggerating the model so that the tree is modelled as a particle 10 m from the base of the tree,

$$2000 \times 10 \times 10 = \tfrac{1}{2} \times 2000 \times (10\omega)^2$$

$$\Rightarrow \omega^2 = 2$$

$$\Rightarrow \omega = 1.4 \text{ rad s}^{-1}$$

The true value would lie between 0.775 and 1.4, so the answer in (a) is an underestimate.

In the second case you might model the tree as a particle at the topmost point.

$$2000 \times 10 \times 50 = \tfrac{1}{2} \times 2000 \times (50\omega)^2$$

$$\Rightarrow \omega^2 = \tfrac{20}{50}$$

$$\Rightarrow \omega = 0.63 \text{ rad s}^{-1}$$

In this case the answer in (a) would be an overestimate.

5.

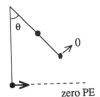

zero PE

Model the rope as a rod. Then its moment of inertia about an axis through one end is:

$$\tfrac{4}{3} \times 20 \times 5^2 = \tfrac{2000}{3} \text{ kg m}^2$$

When the rope is vertical, $\omega = \tfrac{6}{10} = 0.6 \text{ rad s}^{-1}$

Suppose that the greatest angle attained with the vertical is θ.

$$\text{Initial KE} = \tfrac{1}{2} \times \tfrac{2000}{3} \times 0.6^2 + \tfrac{1}{2} \times 25 \times 6^2$$

$$= 120 + 450 = 570 \text{ joules}$$

Gain in PE $= 20g(5 - 5 \cos \theta) + 25g (10 - 10 \cos \theta) = 3500 (1 - \cos \theta)$

Final KE $= 0$

$$570 = 3500 (1 - \cos \theta)$$

$$1 - \cos \theta = \tfrac{570}{3500} \Rightarrow \theta \approx 33°$$

3.4 Parallel axis theorem

Test this theorem using the various moments of inertia of a rod calculated in Example 3.

The moment of inertia of a rod of length $2d$ about an axis through its mid-point perpendicular to the rod is $\frac{Md^2}{3}$. Hence, using the theorem, the moment of inertia about an axis parallel to the first axis and a distance d away should be:

$$\frac{Md^2}{3} + Md^2 = \frac{4}{3}Md^2$$

This confirms result (b).

The moment of inertia of a rod of mass M and length $2d$, about an axis along the length of the rod, is zero. Again using the theorem, the moment of inertia of the rod about an axis parallel to the rod and a distance h away should be $0 + Mh^2 = Mh^2$.

This confirms result (c).

Use the definition of the centre of mass to explain why $\Sigma\, mb \cos \phi = 0$.

Let G be the origin and take the x-axis in the direction $\overrightarrow{GD}$.

Then $\Sigma mb \cos \phi = \Sigma mx = M\,\bar{x}$

$$= 0, \text{ since } \bar{x} = 0.$$

Exercise 4

1. Moment of inertia of a hollow sphere about a diameter is $\frac{2}{3}\,Mr^2$ kg m².

    Moment of inertia of the given sphere is $\frac{2}{3} \times 10 \times 0.15^2 = 0.15$ kg m².

    Moment of inertia about an axis 1 metre from its centre is $0.15 + 10 \times 1^2$
    $$= 10.15 \text{ kg m}^2$$

2. Moment of inertia about diameter $= \frac{2}{5}\,Mr^2 = \frac{2}{5} \times 10 \times 0.15^2 = 0.09$ kg m²

    Moment of inertia about axis 1 metre away is $0.09 + 10 \times 1^2 = 10.09$ kg m²

3. Moment of inertia about axis through centre $= \frac{1}{2}Mr^2 = \frac{1}{8}$ kg m²

    Moment of inertia about axis through point on circumference $= \frac{1}{8} + 1 \times \left(\frac{1}{2}\right)^2$
    $$= \frac{3}{8} \text{ kg m}^2$$

4. (a)  Moment of inertia of a sphere about its centre is

$$\frac{2}{5}Mr^2 = \frac{2}{5} \times 0.1 \times 0.05^2 = 0.0001 \text{ kg m}^2$$

Moment of inertia of sphere about O is

$$0.0001 + 0.1 \times 0.55^2 = 0.030\ 35 \text{ kg m}^2$$

Moment of inertia of rod about O is

$$\frac{1}{3} \times 0.1 \times 0.5^2 = 0.008\ 33 \text{ kg m}^2$$

Moment of inertia of wand is

$$0.030\ 35 + 0.030\ 35 + 0.008\ 33 = 0.069 \text{ kg m}^2$$

(b) Using the parallel axis theorem, the moment of inertia of the wand about a point through the centre of a sphere is:

$$0.069 + 0.3 \times 0.55^2 = 0.160 \text{ kg m}^2$$

5. (a) Moment of inertia of disc about its centre is

$$\frac{Mr^2}{2} = \frac{1}{2} \times 0.2 \times 0.03^2 = 0.000\ 09 \text{ kg m}^2$$

Moment of inertia of disc about O is

$$0.000\ 09 + 0.2 \times 0.8^2 \approx 0.128 \text{ kg m}^2$$

Moment of inertia of rod about axis through O is

$$\frac{4}{3} \times 0.1 \times 0.5^2 \approx 0.033 \text{ kg m}^2$$

Moment of inertia of system about axis through O is

$$0.128 + 0.033 = 0.161 \text{ kg m}^2$$

(b) As the disc moves nearer O, the moment of inertia decreases.

6. Moment of inertia about the axis is 5.5 kg m²

Moment of inertia about parallel axis through centre is

$$5.5 - 12 \times 0.5^2 = 2.5 \text{ kg m}^2$$

Moment of inertia about parallel axis 20 cm from centre is

$$2.5 + 12 \times 0.2^2 = 2.98 \text{ kg m}^2$$

3.5   Perpendicular axes theorem

> **Test this theorem using some of the moments of inertia given in the table in Section 3.2, for example those for the ring and those for the square.**

(a)   Moment of inertia of the ring about a diameter is $\frac{1}{2}Mr^2$.

Moment of inertia of the ring about a perpendicular diameter is $\frac{1}{2}Mr^2$.

So the moment of inertia of the ring about an axis through the centre perpendicular to the ring should be $\frac{1}{2}Mr^2 + \frac{1}{2}Mr^2 = Mr^2$.

(b)   Moment of inertia of square of side $2a$ about an axis in the plane through the centre is $\frac{1}{3}Ma^2$.

Moment of inertia of square of side $2a$ about a perpendicular axis in the plane through the centre is $\frac{1}{3}Ma^2$.

Moment of inertia of square about an axis through the centre perpendicular to the lamina should be $\frac{2}{3}Ma^2$.

Exercise 5

1.

A —————a————— B
| |
| | b
| |
D   C

Moment of inertia about AD is $\frac{1}{3}Ma^2$.

Moment of inertia about AB is $\frac{1}{3}Mb^2$.

So the moment of inertia about an axis through A perpendicular to the lamina is

$$\tfrac{1}{3}Ma^2 + \tfrac{1}{3}Mb^2 = \tfrac{1}{3}M(a^2 + b^2)$$

2.

Moment of inertia of a disc radius r about an axis through its centre perpendicular to the disc is $\frac{1}{2}Mr^2$.

The whole disc from which the quadrant is cut has mass $4 \times 3 = 12$ kg, so its moment of inertia would be $\frac{1}{2} \times 12 \times (0.4)^2 = 0.96$ kg m^2.

Hence the moment of inertia of the quadrant about the same axis is

$$\tfrac{1}{4} \times 0.96 = 0.24 \text{ kg m}^2$$

If the moment of inertia of the quadrant about a straight edge is I kg m², then by the perpendicular axes theorem $2I = 0.24$, so $I = 0.12$.

[Note that the question can be answered more simply using the formula for the moment of inertia of a disc about a diameter.]

3. Area of outside circle is $\pi \times 2^2 = 4\pi$.

Area of inside circle is $\pi \times 1^2 = 1\pi$.

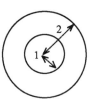

Mass of complete disc is $\frac{4M}{3}$. Mass of disc cut out is $\frac{M}{3}$.

Moment of inertia of complete disc about a perpendicular axis through its centre
is
$$\frac{1}{2} \times \frac{4M}{3} \times 2^2 = \frac{8M}{3}$$

Moment of inertia of disc removed about same axis is
$$\frac{1}{2} \times \frac{M}{3} \times 1^2 = \frac{M}{6}$$

Moment of inertia of washer is
$$\frac{8M}{3} - \frac{M}{6} = \frac{5}{2}M$$

If the moment of inertia of the washer about a diameter is I, then $\frac{5}{2}M = I + I$ by
the perpendicular axes theorem. Hence the moment of inertia of the washer about
a diameter is $\frac{5}{4}M$.

[Again, the question can be solved without using the perpendicular axes theorem.]

4. (a)

Moment of inertia of disc about the axis is
$$\frac{1}{2} \times 0.03 \times 0.08^2 + 0.03 \times 0.18^2 = 0.001\ 068$$

Moment of inertia of rod about the axis is
$$\frac{4}{3} \times 0.03 \times 0.05^2 = 0.0001$$

Total moment of inertia = $0.001\ 168$ kg m^2

Initial PE = $0.03 \times 10 \times 0.18 + 0.03 \times 10 \times 0.05 = 0.069$

Final PE = 0

Initial KE = 0   Final KE = $\frac{1}{2}I\omega^2$

Assuming mechanical energy is conserved,
$$0.069 = \frac{1}{2} \times 0.001\ 168\omega^2$$
$$\Rightarrow \omega^2 = 118.15$$
$$\Rightarrow \omega = 10.9 \text{ rad s}^{-1}$$

(b)

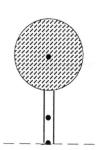

Moment of inertia of disc about the axis is

$$\frac{0.03}{4} \times 0.08^2 + 0.03 \times 0.18^2 = 0.001\ 02 \text{ kg m}^2$$

Moment of inertia of rod about the axis is 0.0001 kg m^2

Total moment of inertia $= 0.001\ 12$ kg m^2

Assuming mechanical energy is conserved,

$$0.069 = \frac{1}{2} \times 0.001\ 12\omega^2$$

$$\Rightarrow \omega^2 = 123.2$$

$$\Rightarrow \omega = 11.1 \text{ rad s}^{-1}$$

The bat should fall fastest when allowed to fall in this way. In fact, air resistance will not be negligible in this case and so the model would need to be modified.

4 *Rotation and angular acceleration*

4.1 Moment of momentum – angular momentum

Exercise 1

1.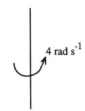

Angular momentum before $= I\omega = 4I$

Angular momentum after $= \frac{3}{4} I\omega_1$

Angular momentum is conserved, so

$$\frac{3}{4} I\omega_1 = 4I$$
$$\omega_1 = \frac{16}{3} \text{ rad s}^{-1}$$

Initial energy $= \frac{1}{2} I\omega^2 = 8I$

Final energy $= \frac{1}{2} \times \frac{3}{4} I \times \omega_1^2 = \frac{32}{3} I$

Work done $= \frac{8}{3} I$

2. (a) Initial angular momentum $= I\omega = 40$
   Final angular momentum $= 8\omega_1$
   $$\omega_1 = 5 \text{ rad s}^{-1}$$

   The cake and turntable spin at an angular speed of 5 rads s^{-1}.

   (b) If the table were completely smooth the cake would remain stationary while the turntable would spin around underneath with an angular speed of 10 rad s^{-1}.

3. Initial angular momentum $= 0.1 \times \frac{78 \times 2\pi}{60}$

   Angular momentum with n records $= (0.1 + 0.02n) \times \omega_n$,

   where ω_n is angular speed.

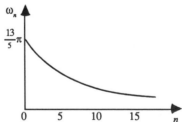

Since angular speed is conserved,

$$\omega_n = \frac{0.1 \times 78 \times 2\pi}{60 (0.1 + 0.02n)}$$

$$= \frac{13\pi}{(5 + n)}$$

4.2   Acceleration of a particle moving in a circle

> (a)   What is meant by $\ddot{\theta}$ and $\dot{\theta}$?
>
> (b)   Write down as a column vector the position vector of P relative to O .
>
> (c)   Confirm by differentiation that the acceleration of P has components $r\dot{\theta}^2$ in the direction $\overrightarrow{PO}$ and $r\ddot{\theta}$ tangentially in the direction of increasing θ.

(a) $\dot{\theta} = \dfrac{d\theta}{dt}$, the angular velocity of P

$\ddot{\theta} = \dfrac{d^2\theta}{dt^2}$, the angular acceleration of P

(b)   The position vector of P is $\mathbf{r} = \begin{bmatrix} r\cos\theta \\ r\sin\theta \end{bmatrix} = r\begin{bmatrix} \cos\theta \\ \sin\theta \end{bmatrix}$

(c)   To obtain the acceleration, differentiate $\mathbf{r}$ twice with respect to time. The radius r is constant.

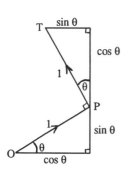

$\dot{\mathbf{r}} = r\begin{bmatrix} -\sin\theta\,\dot{\theta} \\ \cos\theta\,\dot{\theta} \end{bmatrix} = r\dot{\theta}\begin{bmatrix} -\sin\theta \\ \cos\theta \end{bmatrix}$

The two vectors $\begin{bmatrix} \cos\theta \\ \sin\theta \end{bmatrix}$ and $\begin{bmatrix} -\sin\theta \\ \cos\theta \end{bmatrix}$ which occur in the expressions for $\mathbf{r}$ and $\dot{\mathbf{r}}$ are both unit vectors. The first is directed radially outwards and the second is at a right angle to this in the direction of increasing θ (the vectors $\overrightarrow{OP}$ and $\overrightarrow{PT}$ in the diagram).

The acceleration $\ddot{\mathbf{r}} = r\dot{\theta}\begin{bmatrix} -\cos\theta\,\dot{\theta} \\ -\sin\theta\,\dot{\theta} \end{bmatrix} + r\ddot{\theta}\begin{bmatrix} -\sin\theta \\ \cos\theta \end{bmatrix}$

$= -r\dot{\theta}^2\begin{bmatrix} \cos\theta \\ \sin\theta \end{bmatrix} + r\ddot{\theta}\begin{bmatrix} -\sin\theta \\ \cos\theta \end{bmatrix}$

$\ddot{\mathbf{r}}$ has a component $r\dot{\theta}^2$ in the direction PO and a component $r\ddot{\theta}$ tangentially in the direction of increasing θ.

Exercise 2

1. $r = 0.1$, $\theta = 3t^2 \Rightarrow \dot{\theta} = 6t$ and $\ddot{\theta} = 6$

   The radial and tangential components of the acceleration of P are $3.6t^2$ m s^{-2} towards O and 0.6 m s^{-2} in the direction of increasing θ.

   When $t = 1$, the components are 3.6 m s^{-2} and 0.6 m s^{-2}.
   When $t = 3$, the components are 32.4 m s^{-2} and 0.6 m s^{-2}.

   The heavy weight has the same acceleration as the tangential component of P, i.e. 0.6 m s^{-2} downwards.

2. $\theta = 1 + 3\sin t \Rightarrow \dot{\theta} = 3\cos t$, $\ddot{\theta} = -3\sin t$

   Velocity $= r\dot{\theta} = 5 \times 3\cos 2 = -6.24$ m s^{-1}

   Radial acceleration: $r\dot{\theta}^2 = -5 \times 9\cos^2 2 = 7.79$ m s^{-2}

   Tangential acceleration: $r\ddot{\theta} = 5 \times -3\sin 2 = -13.64$ m s^{-2}

   The angle between the velocity and the acceleration is:

   $$\tan^{-1} \frac{7.79}{13.64} = 30° \text{ (to the nearest degree)}$$

3. $r = 15$, $r\ddot{\theta} = 2$, $r\dot{\theta} = 10 \Rightarrow r\dot{\theta}^2 = \frac{10^2}{15} = \frac{20}{3}$

   $a = \sqrt{\left(2^2 + \left(\frac{20}{3}\right)^2\right)} \approx 6.96$

   $\tan^{-1}\left(\frac{10}{3}\right) \approx 73°$

   The acceleration of the motor-cylist is 6.96 m s^{-2} at an angle 73° below the horizontal.

4. (a) Speed $= v = r\dot{\theta}$

   If r is constant, the rate of change of speed is $\frac{dv}{dt} = r\ddot{\theta}$. Thus the tangential component of the acceleration is the rate of change of speed.

   The radial component is $r\dot{\theta}^2 = \frac{1}{r}(r\dot{\theta})^2 = \frac{v^2}{r}$.

   So the acceleration components are $-\frac{v^2}{r}$ radially and $\frac{dv}{dt}$ tangentially.

   (b) If the acceleration is wholly radial, $\frac{dv}{dt} = 0$ and the speed is constant.

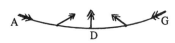

   The angle between the radius and the acceleration decreases from 90° at A where the speed is zero, to 0° at D and to $-90°$ at G where the speed is again zero.

x

4.3   The equation for rotational motion

> **What do the variables S, T and C represent in the model?**

S is the force on the drawbridge from the axis about which the drawbridge is rotating.
T is the tension in the cables.
C is the frictional couple at the axis which is the result of the frictional forces opposing the rotational motion.

Exercise 3

1. $KE = \frac{1}{2}I\dot{\theta}^2 = \frac{1}{2} \times 45 \times 4^2$

   $\qquad = 360$ joules

   Angular momentum $= I\dot{\theta}$

   $\qquad\qquad = 45 \times 4 = 180$ kg m² s⁻¹

2.

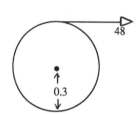

   $I\ddot{\theta} = \Sigma Fr$

   $\Rightarrow 18\ddot{\theta} = 48 \times 0.3$

   $\qquad \ddot{\theta} = 0.8$ rad s⁻²

   $\Rightarrow \qquad \dot{\theta} = 0.8t + 2$, as $\dot{\theta} = 2$ when $t = 0$

   When $t = 5$, $\dot{\theta} = 6$

   The angular speed is 6 rad s⁻¹ after 5 seconds.

3.

   $I\ddot{\theta} = C$

   $\Rightarrow 60\ddot{\theta} = C$

   $\dot{\theta} = \frac{C}{60} \times t \quad$ as $\dot{\theta} = 0$ when $t = 0$

   $\Rightarrow \theta = \frac{C}{120}t^2 \quad$ as $\theta = 0$ when $t = 0$

   $\Rightarrow \theta = \frac{C}{120}\left(\frac{60\dot{\theta}}{C}\right)^2$

   $\qquad = \frac{30\dot{\theta}^2}{C}$

   After 200 revolutions, $\dot{\theta} = 20 \times 2\pi$ rad s⁻¹, so

   $\qquad 200 \times 2\pi = \frac{30 \times 40^2 \times \pi^2}{C}$

   $\qquad \Rightarrow \quad C = 120\pi$ Nm

4. $I\ddot{\theta} = -C \Rightarrow \ddot{\theta} = -\dfrac{C}{500}$

$\Rightarrow \dot{\theta} = \dfrac{-Ct}{500} + A$ where A is a constant

When $t = 25$, $\dot{\theta} = 0$.

Therefore $-\dfrac{C \times 25}{500} + A = 0 \Rightarrow A = \dfrac{C}{20}$

Hence $\dot{\theta} = \dfrac{C}{500}(25 - t)$

When $t = 0$, $\dot{\theta} = \dfrac{100 \times 2\pi}{60}$

Therefore $\dfrac{100 \times 2\pi}{60} = \dfrac{C}{20}$

$C = \dfrac{200\pi}{3}$ Nm

5.

Let the angular acceleration be $\ddot{\theta}$.

Then for the cylinder, $Ta = I\ddot{\theta}$

$= 3ma^2\ddot{\theta}$

$T = 3ma\ddot{\theta}$

For the mass, $ma\ddot{\theta} = mg - T$

Hence $4ma\ddot{\theta} = mg$

$\Rightarrow a\ddot{\theta} = \dfrac{1}{4}g$

The acceleration of P is $\dfrac{1}{4}g$.

6.

Let the angular acceleration be $\ddot{\theta}$, as shown.

For the pulley, $I\ddot{\theta} = 0.1T_2 - 0.1T_1$

$\Rightarrow \ddot{\theta} = T_2 - T_1$ ①

For mass A, $20 - T_2 = 2 \times 0.1\ddot{\theta} \Rightarrow T_2 = 20 - 0.2\ddot{\theta}$ ②

For mass B, $T_1 - 10 = 1 \times 0.1\ddot{\theta} \Rightarrow T_1 = 10 + 0.1\ddot{\theta}$ ③

Substituting for T_2 and T_1 from ② and ③ into ①,

$\ddot{\theta} = 20 - 0.2\ddot{\theta} - 10 - 0.1\ddot{\theta}$

$\Rightarrow 1.3\ddot{\theta} = 10$

$\Rightarrow \ddot{\theta} = 7.7$ rad s^{-2}

5 *Modelling with rigid bodies*

5.1 The force at the pivot

> **What external forces act on the pirate ship?**

The main forces acting on the ship are its weight, acting vertically downwards and the force at the pivot point. Air resistance can probably be ignored.

The weight, Mg, can be modelled as acting through the centre of mass of the boat, G.

There may also be a frictional couple at the pivot point.

> For a single particle, $m\ddot{\mathbf{r}} = \dfrac{d^2}{dt^2}(m\mathbf{r})$
>
> (a) For the two particles m_1 and m_2 show that:
>
> $$\sum \frac{d^2}{dt^2}(m\mathbf{r}) = \frac{d^2}{dt^2}\left(\sum m\mathbf{r}\right)$$
>
> (b) What is the formula for the position vector $\mathbf{r}_G$ of the centre of mass?

(a) $\quad \dfrac{d^2(m_1\mathbf{r}_1 + m_2\mathbf{r}_2)}{dt^2} = \dfrac{d^2(m_1\mathbf{r}_1)}{dt^2} + \dfrac{d^2(m_2\mathbf{r}_2)}{dt^2}$

$\Rightarrow \quad \dfrac{d^2\sum m\mathbf{r}}{dt^2} = \sum\dfrac{d^2(m\mathbf{r})}{dt^2}$

(b) The position vector of the centre of mass is:

$$\mathbf{r}_G = \frac{\sum m\mathbf{r}}{\sum m} = \frac{\sum m\mathbf{r}}{M}$$

Exercise 1

In some examples you may find it easier not to substitute values for the variables until the end of your answer.

1.

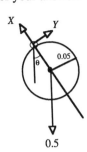

When the bauble is in its highest position, $\dot{\theta} = 0$.

Since $X - mg \cos \theta = ma\,\dot{\theta}^2$

$X = mg \cos \theta = 0.5 \cos 20° = 0.470$ newton

For a hollow sphere about a point on the surface, $I = \frac{2}{3}ma^2 + ma^2 = \frac{5}{3}ma^2$

So $I\ddot{\theta} = -mga \sin \theta \quad \Rightarrow \quad \ddot{\theta} = -\dfrac{3g \sin \theta}{5a}$

Now $\qquad\qquad Y - mg \sin \theta = ma\ddot{\theta}$

$$= -\frac{3mg \sin \theta}{5}$$

$$Y = \frac{2mg \sin \theta}{5} = 0.2 \sin 20° = 0.068 \text{ newtons}$$

The total reaction force is $\sqrt{(X^2 + Y^2)} = \sqrt{0.475}$ newton.

2. (a)

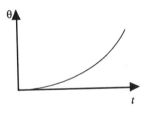

t (s)	θ (rad)
0.0	0.000
1.1	0.175
1.5	0.349
2.1	0.698
2.6	1.047
3.0	1.396

The formula $\theta = 0.15t^2$ fits the data quite well. You might find a more accurate value for the constant.

(b) $\dot{\theta} = 0.3t \Rightarrow \ddot{\theta} = 0.3$

(c) The moment of inertia of a rectangular lamina about a line in the plane of the lamina and through its centre of gravity is $\frac{1}{3}Ma^2$ where $2a$ is the width of the lamina. By the parallel axis theorem, the moment of inertia about a line 0.2 m from the edge is: $\frac{1}{3} \times 40 \times 0.6^2 + 40 \times 0.4^2 = 11.2$ kg m^2

$$C = 11.2\ddot{\theta} = 3.36 \text{ Nm}$$

(d) $\frac{1}{2}I\dot{\theta}^2 = C\theta$

$$\Rightarrow \dot{\theta} = \sqrt{\left(\frac{2C\theta}{I}\right)} = \sqrt{\left(\frac{2 \times 3.36 \times 1.396}{11.2}\right)} = 0.92 \text{ rad s}^{-1}$$

3.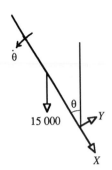

When $t = 0$, $\theta = \frac{\pi}{6}$ and $\dot\theta = 0$

$$I\ddot\theta = 15\,000 \times 2 \sin\theta$$

$$\Rightarrow \ddot\theta = \frac{1}{8000} \times 15\,000 \times 2 \sin\theta$$

$$\Rightarrow \ddot\theta = \frac{15}{4} \sin\theta$$

$mg \sin\theta - Y = ma\ddot\theta$

$$\Rightarrow Y = 15\,000 \sin\theta - \frac{1500 \times 15}{2} \sin\theta = 3750 \sin\theta$$

When $\theta = 45°$, $Y = 2652$ newtons

Taking the plane through the base as zero potential level,

when $\theta = 30°$, $KE = 0$, $\qquad PE = 2 \cos 30° \times 15\,000$

when $\theta = 45°$, $KE = 0.5I\dot\theta^2$, $\qquad PE = 2 \cos 45° \times 15\,000$

Assuming that energy is conserved,

$$0.5I\dot\theta^2 + 30\,000 \cos 45° = 30\,000 \cos 30°$$

$$4000\dot\theta^2 = 30\,000 (\cos 30° - \cos 45°)$$

$$\dot\theta^2 = 1.1919$$

$$\dot\theta = 1.09 \text{ rad s}^{-1}$$

$$X + mg \cos\theta = ma\dot\theta^2$$

$$X + 15\,000 \cos\theta = 30000\dot\theta^2$$

So when $\theta = 45°$, $\qquad X = 3000 \times 1.1919 - 15\,000 \cos 45°$

$$= -7031 \text{ newtons}$$

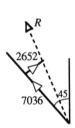

Then $\sqrt{(X^2 + Y^2)} \approx 7515$

The resultant force is 7515 newtons acting at angle 24.3° to the vertical.

4.

$$\theta = 0.2 \sin 2\pi t$$

$$\dot\theta = 0.4\pi \cos 2\pi t$$

$$\ddot\theta = -0.8\pi^2 \sin 2\pi t = -4\pi^2\theta$$

By Newton's second law, $Y - mg \sin\theta = ma\ddot\theta$

$$Y - 20 \sin\theta = -1.4 \times 4\pi^2\theta$$

$$Y = 20 \sin\theta - 55.3\,\theta$$

$$X - mg \cos\theta = ma\dot\theta^2$$

$$X - 20 \cos\theta = 1.4 \times 0.16\pi^2 \cos^2 2\pi t$$

$$= 1.4 \times 0.16\pi^2 \left[1 - \left(\frac{\theta}{0.2}\right)^2 \right]$$

$$X = 20 \cos\theta + 2.21 - 55.3\,\theta^2$$

When $\theta = 0.1745$ radian, $Y = -6.2$ newtons and $X = 20.2$ newtons.

5E. | **Set up a model**

The ruler is taken to be a uniform rod. The only forces acting are gravity and the contact force at the table. This has components X newtons along the rod and Y newtons perpendicular to the rod as shown. The friction force is sufficient to prevent slipping.

| **Analyse**

(a) (i) $\qquad I\ddot{\theta} = 0.6 \times 0.15 \sin\theta = 0.09 \sin\theta$

$\qquad$ But $\quad I = \dfrac{4}{3} \times 0.06 \times 0.15^2$

$\qquad \Rightarrow \quad \ddot{\theta} = 50 \sin\theta$

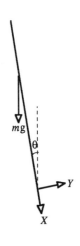

(ii) $\qquad \ddot{\theta} = \dot{\theta}\dfrac{d\dot{\theta}}{d\theta} \Rightarrow \int\ddot{\theta}\,d\theta = \int\dot{\theta}\,d\dot{\theta}$

$\qquad$ So $\int 50 \sin\theta\,d\theta = \int\dot{\theta}\,d\dot{\theta}$

$\qquad\qquad -50\cos\theta = \dfrac{1}{2}\dot{\theta}^2 + C$

$\qquad$ Since $\dot{\theta} = 0$ when $\theta = 0, C = -50$

$\qquad\qquad \dfrac{1}{2}\dot{\theta}^2 = 50\,(1 - \cos\theta)$

$\qquad\qquad \dot{\theta} = 10\sqrt{(1 - \cos\theta)}$

(b) When $\theta = 15°$, $\ddot{\theta} = 12.9$ and $\dot{\theta} = 1.85$

By Newton's second law,

$X + mg\cos\theta = ma\dot{\theta}^2$

$\qquad\qquad X = 0.06 \times 0.15 \times 1.85^2 - 0.6\cos 15°$

$\qquad\qquad\quad = -0.549$ newton

$mg\sin\theta - Y = ma\ddot{\theta}$

$\qquad\qquad Y = 0.6\sin 15° - 0.06 \times 0.15 \times 12.9$

$\qquad\qquad\quad = 0.039$ newton

The contact force P is 0.55 newton at an angle of $75° + 4° = 79°$ to the horizontal.

(c) The normal reaction is $R = P\cos 11°$.

The friction force is $F = P\sin 11°$.

When friction is limiting, $F = \mu R$

i.e. $\sin 11° = \mu\cos 11°$

So the least value of μ to avoid slipping is $\tan 11° = 0.19$.

5.2   Modelling rigid body motion

> Which of the situations below can you model as:
>
> (a)   particle motion;
>
> (b)   rigid body motion about a fixed axis;
>
> (c)   a rigid body in equilibrium?

The diver

The motion of the centre of mass of the diver can be modelled as that of a particle. A more sophisticated model, involving rotation about a moving centre of mass, would be needed to describe the motion of the diver's body relative to the centre of mass.

The pot

Once the pot has assumed its final shape, its motion will be described extremely well by the theory of rigid body motion about a fixed axis.

The stilt walker

Whilst the walker is taking a step (or toppling over), the motion is likely to be modelled well by rigid body motion about a fixed axis. Whilst the performer is standing still, results concerning rigid body equilibrium could be applied (and should show that equilibrium is unstable!)

The gymnast

Rigid body motion about an axis through the gymnast's shoulder would describe the motion in the picture reasonably well.

The trapeze artist

A particle model would probably suffice but a better model would be a rigid body (a uniform rod) on the end of a string.